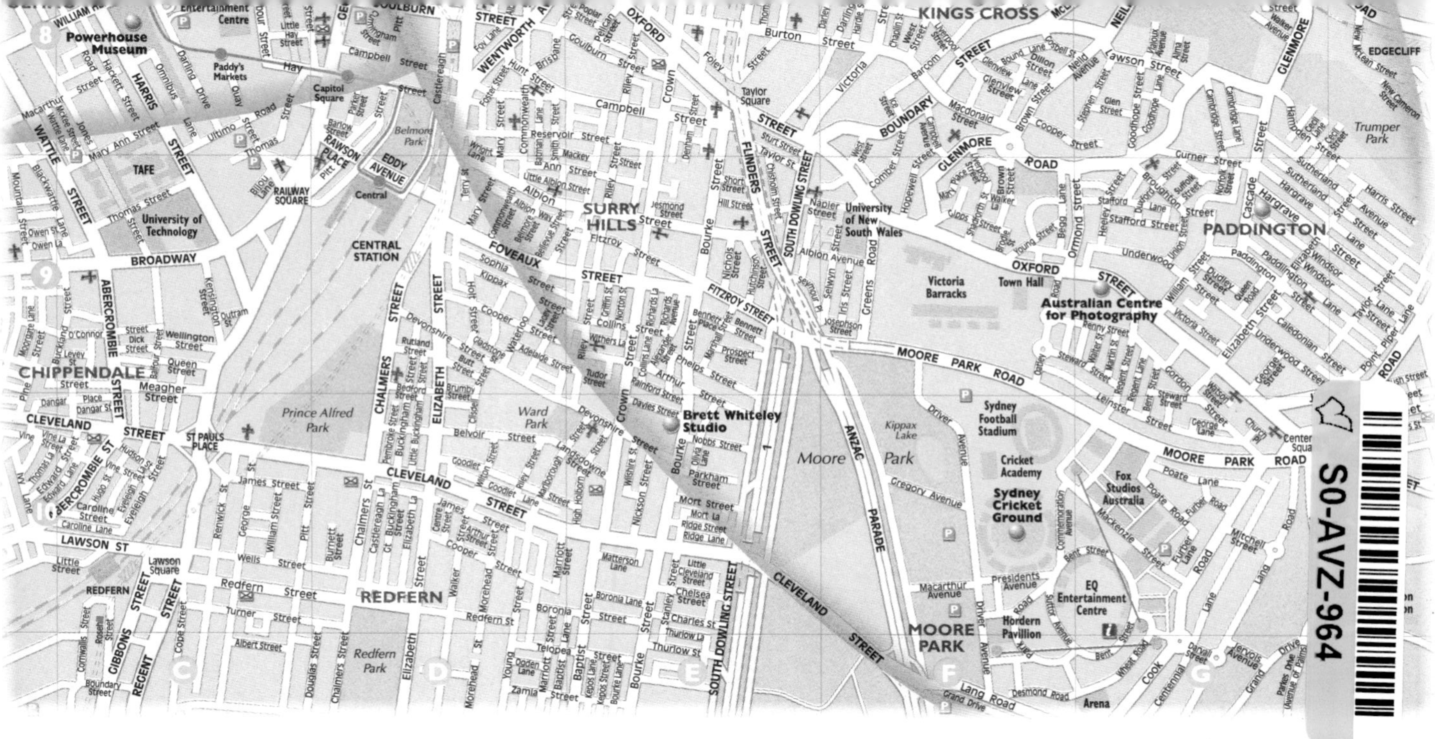

KINGS CROSS
PADDINGTON
EDGECLIFF
SURRY HILLS
MOORE PARK
REDFERN
CHIPPENDALE
Trumper Park
Australian Centre for Photography
Town Hall
Victoria Barracks
University of New South Wales
Sydney Football Stadium
Cricket Academy
Sydney Cricket Ground
Fox Studios Australia
EQ Entertainment Centre
Hordern Pavillion
Arena
Kippax Lake
Moore Park
Taylor Square
Brett Whiteley Studio
Ward Park
CENTRAL STATION
Central
Belmore Park
Capitol Square
Prince Alfred Park
Redfern Park
Paddy's Markets
Entertainment Centre
Powerhouse Museum
TAFE
University of Technology
RAILWAY SQUARE
OXFORD STREET
FLINDERS STREET
SOUTH DOWLING STREET
MOORE PARK ROAD
ANZAC PARADE
CLEVELAND STREET
ELIZABETH STREET
CHALMERS STREET
EDDY AVENUE
RAWSON PLACE
BROADWAY
HARRIS STREET
WATTLE STREET
ABERCROMBIE STREET
REGENT STREET
GIBBONS STREET
LAWSON ST
8
9
10
C
D
E
F
G

How to Use This Book

KEY TO SYMBOLS

- Map reference to the accompanying fold-out map
- Address
- Telephone number
- Opening/closing times
- Restaurant or café
- Nearest rail station
- Nearest subway (Metro) station
- Nearest bus route
- Nearest riverboat or ferry stop
- Facilities for visitors with disabilities
- Other practical information
- Further information
- Tourist information
- Admission charges: Expensive (over A$20) Moderate (A$10–A$20) Inexpensive (A$10 or less)

This guide is divided into four sections

• Essential Sydney: An introduction to the city and tips on making the most of your stay.

• Sydney by Area: We've broken the city into five areas, and recommended the best sights, shops, entertainment venues, nightlife and restaurants in each one. Suggested walks help you to explore on foot.

• Where to Stay: The best hotels, whether you're looking for luxury, budget or something in between.

• Need to Know: The info you need to make your trip run smoothly, including getting about by public transport, weather tips, emergency phone numbers and useful websites.

Navigation In the Sydney by Area chapter, we've given each area its own color, which is also used on the locator maps throughout the book and the map on the inside front cover.

Maps The fold-out map accompanying this book is a comprehensive street plan of Sydney. The grid on this fold-out map is the same as the grid on the locator maps within the book. We've given grid references within the book for each sight and listing.

Contents

Introducing Sydney

Cosmopolitan, diverse, energetic and easygoing, Sydney has colonial heritage, dazzling modern buildings and a free-wheeling lifestyle. Its iconic, glorious sheltered port and its sunny, subtropical climate help make it a major tourist destination.

Sydney is clean, unpolluted and relatively safe, and it's not surprising that it is most often voted as one of the world's most liveable cities. But, far from being the clichéd sun, sand, surf and sport scene you might expect, Sydney also has world-class museums and galleries as well as a roster of shops that include branches of luxury brands such as Tiffany and Cartier. The cuisine is truly superb—Sydney is now one of the modern food capitals of the world—plus there are many excellent Australian wines.

After dark you can take in an opera or ballet at the Sydney Opera House, see a first-class theatrical production, dance the night away in a classy pub, take in the sparkling vistas from a vantage point such as Sydney Tower, or spend the evening sampling local beer in a historic sandstone hotel at Sydney's birthplace, The Rocks.

A vibrant world business capital, Sydney has a commercial buzz that permeates the Central Business District (CBD). The city embraces people of all races and nationalities and, although this doesn't make it a multicultural utopia, you get the feeling that you are visiting an international destination. An Asian presence is strong, and you'll overhear any number of European languages.

The pace in Sydney is faster than in other parts of Australia, so the nasally Australian English, with its distinctive colloquialisms, is delivered double time. The often-heard expressions "No worries, mate" and "She'll be right" say much about the attitudes here. Come to Sydney with an open mind, meet people halfway, take Sydney as it comes, and you're bound to have a relaxing and thoroughly good time.

Facts + Figures

- From 1,400 people in 1788, Sydney's population has grown to more than 4 million people.
- Around 70 percent of Sydneysiders are a combination of at least two ethnic backgrounds, while 40 percent are foreign-born.

FAMOUS SYDNEYSIDERS

Heading overseas to hit the big time is an Australian tradition. Among Sydney's most famous exports are supermodel Elle Macpherson, actors Mel Gibson and Cate Blanchett, author and TV personality Clive James, and art critic Robert Hughes. Although actress Nicole Kidman left her place of birth, Hawaii, at four years, she considers herself an honorary Sydneysider.

THE DIASPORA

Nearly one million Australians—5 percent of the population—live and/or work in other countries. These people have been quiet achievers in Asian countries such as Singapore and China for many years. The diaspora actually promotes Australia's commercial interests, and when these people return, they bring new skills and new experiences to the workplace.

ABORIGINAL PRESENCE

Aborigines have lived on the Australian mainland for over 60,000 years and many of their descendants live in Sydney. Indigenous arts and crafts are mostly made by people who live elsewhere in the country, particularly northern Australia. The remains of Aboriginal culture in Sydney consist of shell middens on the Harbour foreshores, rock carvings in the surrounding national parks, and in original place names such as Woolloomooloo, Turramurra and Parramatta.

A Short Stay in Sydney

DAY 1

Morning Have an early breakfast and walk to the **Royal Botanic Gardens** (▷ 24–25) for a quiet stroll around the grounds. You might detour to Mrs Macquarie's Point from where you have a classic vista of the **Sydney Opera House** (▷ 30–31) and **Sydney Harbour Bridge** (▷ 27).

Mid-morning Hop on a ferry for a tour of the Harbour. You could go to **Taronga Zoo** (▷ 32–33), or take the public ferry to **Manly** (▷ 95) from where you could make the short walk to **Manly Sea Life Sanctuary** (▷ 95) or head for Manly Beach via the Esplanade.

Lunch Have lunch on the Manly Wharf or take the ferry back to **Circular Quay** (▷ 46) and catch a bus along George Street to **Chinatown** (▷ 56–57) for a meal. The streets around here are worth exploring for interesting Asian curios and exotic food ingredients.

Afternoon After a look around Chinatown, take a walk to **Darling Harbour** (▷ 60–61) and view the marine exhibits at **Sea Life Sydney Aquarium** (▷ 60–61) before heading to the **National Maritime Museum** (▷ 58) via the Harbourside shopping complex.

Dinner Take the Light Rail and venture back into the CBD. Here you'll find an array of dining options, some with city views. If you are looking for budget meals, try one of the excellent food courts in the big retail complexes here.

Evening Take in a performance at the **Opera House** (▷ 30–31) where you can choose from a range of opera, musical and drama performances. Be sure to walk around the Harbour foreshore afterward for stunning city and Harbour views.

DAY 2

Morning Walk from Circular Quay to **The Rocks** (▷ 44–45). You could stop for a look at the **Museum of Contemporary Art** (▷ 40–41) or continue to the BridgeClimb terminus for a morning climb on the **Sydney Harbour Bridge** (▷ 27).

Mid-morning Walk to the elegant **Queen Victoria Building** (▷ 80) where you can shop for brand-name clothing and quality souvenirs. The lower ground floor has a food court, which makes for a great stop for morning coffee or tea.

Lunch Walk to nearby **Hyde Park** (▷ 80) for a picnic lunch on the grass. Afterward you could walk to Macquarie Street to see the **Hyde Park Barracks** (▷ 75), where you'll get a feeling for Sydney's convict past. Just opposite is the historic St. James Church, which dates from 1824.

Afternoon Then walk down Macquarie Street past **State Parliament House** (▷ 81) and the **State Library** (▷ 81) to **Circular Quay** (▷ 46) for a coffee. You may have time to divert into the **Royal Botanic Gardens** (▷ 24–25) for a stroll through this amazing plant collection.

Dinner Dine at **Cafe Sydney** (▷ 51) at Customs House or perhaps at the famed **Sailors Thai** (▷ 52) at nearby The Rocks. The narrow streets here give some of the feeling of old Sydney Town and there are several interesting old pubs.

Evening There are some great nightspots around the city—**The Basement** (▷ 50) is good if you like jazz. Finish the day with a drink on the 36th floor of the Shangri-la Hotel at the **Blu Bar on 36** (▷ 50).

Top 25

TOP 25

Art Gallery of New South Wales ▷ 72 Contains some of Australia's most admired works of art.

Australian Museum ▷ 70–71 An excellent collection of cultural and scientific exhibits.

Bondi Beach ▷ 94 This crescent of sandy beach is a popular hot summer's day destination.

Centennial Park ▷ 73 Rolling lawns, pretty ponds, plus good walking and cycleways.

Chinese Garden and Chinatown ▷ 56–57 The vibrant Asian core of the city.

City Centre ▷ 74 The energetic business hub of Australia is also a retail and dining mecca.

Hyde Park Barracks ▷ 75 Shows what transportees experienced in the early days.

Manly and Manly Sea Life Sanctuary ▷ 95 View the diverse marine life and dive with sharks.

Museum of Contemporary Art ▷ 40–41 Cutting-edge contemporary art.

Museum of Sydney ▷ 42 Sydney's past, well displayed in intimate galleries.

National Maritime Museum ▷ 58 The nation's marine history and a moored submarine.

Paddington ▷ 76–77 Walk the backstreets in this suburb of terraced houses.

Powerhouse Museum ▷ 59 One of Australia's best collections of technology and decorative arts can be found here.

The Rocks ▷ 44–45 Sydney's birthplace, with its old architecture, is well worth exploring.

Royal Botanic Gardens and the Domain ▷ 24–25 Stroll here and have a picnic.

Sea Life Sydney Aquarium and Darling Harbour ▷ 60–61 Sharks and rays, and more from the Great Barrier Reef.

Sydney Harbour ▷ 26 The iconic focal point of the city and the reference point for all attractions.

Sydney Harbour Bridge ▷ 27 Climb this icon for 360-degree views of the city—then tell your friends.

Sydney Harbour National Park ▷ 28–29 This collection of reserves are accessible by ferry.

Sydney Observatory ▷ 43 A working observatory that doubles as a museum of astronomy.

Sydney Olympic Park ▷ 96–97 Home of the 2000 Olympics and a focal point for sports of all kinds.

Sydney Opera House ▷ 30–31 This world architectural icon is the hub of Sydney's performance arts.

Sydney Tower and Skywalk ▷ 78 Come on a fine day for the views, stay for a meal, and dare to take the Skywalk experience.

Taronga Zoo ▷ 32–33 Home to the full range of Australia's wildlife, plus views of the Harbour and the CBD.

Vaucluse House and Vaucluse ▷ 98–99 Heritage-listed mansion, set in well-tended gardens.

These pages are a quick guide to the Top 25, which are described in more detail later. Here they are listed alphabetically, and the tinted background shows which area they are in.

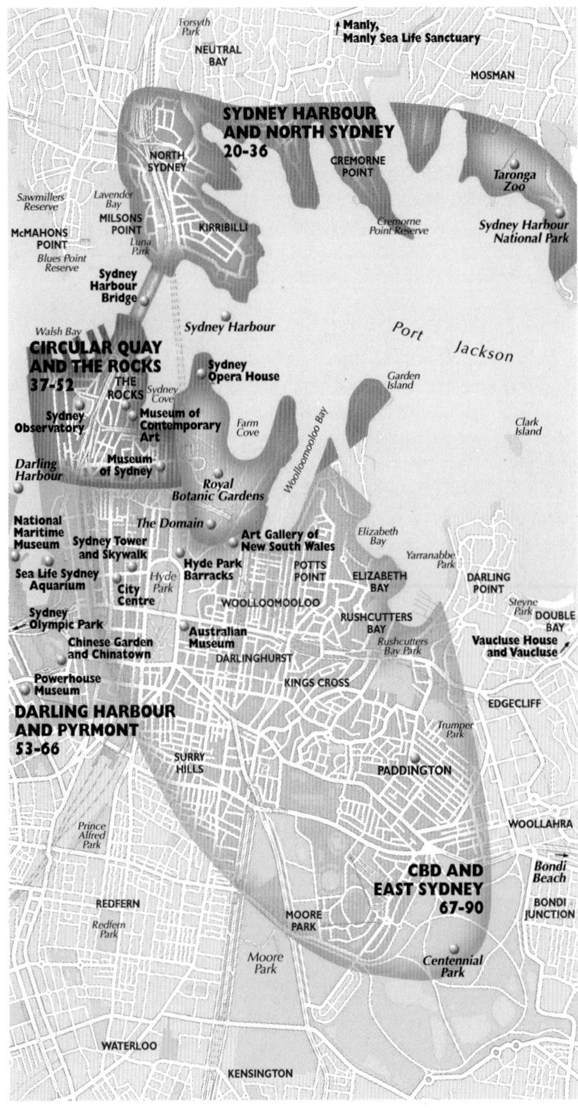

Shopping

Apart from having the usual swag of international brand-name retail outlets, Sydney has many shops selling designer clothing, original arts and crafts and stunning gemstone jewelry.

A Memento

Visitors keen to take home a memento tend to go for an item of Australiana such as diamond, opal or pearl jewelry; Akubra stockmen's hats; outback clothing; Drizabone rainware; kangaroo or crocodile leather products; or exquisite craft objects in glass, wood, porcelain and silver inspired by Australian nature.

Aussie Wares

The range of Aboriginal arts and crafts is enormous. But try to distinguish between handmade craft items derived from distinct Aboriginal settlements and the mundane, generic goods that are mass produced and have no authenticity. Look out for the signed traditional bowls, didgeridoos, boomerangs and wood carvings. Art enthusiasts go for the Arnhem Land bark paintings and Central Australian dot paintings. Seek out a reputable gallery and ask questions regarding provenance and authenticity. Original Australian design brands to look out for include Ken Done, featuring bright, vibrant clothing, homewares, bags, prints and jewelry, and Mambo with surf and streetwear featuring funky designs. There are several local store chains selling goods that are not found internationally, including the Australian Geographic Shop (▷ 104),

There are plenty of shopping opportunities in Sydney's individual shops, shopping malls and arcades

MUSEUM SHOPS

At the Art Gallery of New South Wales (▷ 72), you'll find Sydney's best selection of art books and cards. The Museum of Contemporary Art (▷ 40–41) offers jewelry, design objects and books inspired by Australian designers. The shop at the Australian Museum (▷ 70–71) focuses on Australian nature books. The Australian Centre for Photography (▷ 79) showcases local talent.

offering environmentally friendly goods, Australian nature books and outdoor clothing; and the ABC Shop (▷ 84), operated by the Australian Broadcasting Corporation, selling books, audio and video products, and toys relating to popular local TV shows.

Food and Drink

Those who have sampled the widely exported Aussie wines will be impressed with the huge range on offer. While the major grape varieties from regions such as the Hunter Barossa and Yarra Valleys are well known, look for Margaret River and Clare Valley wines; also check out the newest grape varieties Verdelho and Petit Verdo. And finally, if you must impress friends back home with an item not found elsewhere, pick up a macadamia nut cracker. Normally sold with a bunch of nuts to crack, this threaded screw device cracks the shells of Australia's major contribution to the world's food stocks. The best place in the city to sample Australian foods is at the lower ground-floor food hall of the David Jones department store in Market Street (▷ 85). Here you'll find wonderful produce including delicatessen lines, Aussie wines and beers, cheeses, meats, seafood, fruits and vegetables.

AUSTRALIAN GEMS AND JEWELRY

Sydney is internationally renowned for the range and quality of its opal, pearl and other gemstone jewelry. The best shops feature original designs utilizing multicolored opals, lustrous South Sea pearls and exquisite Argyle diamonds in white, pink and champagne shades. You can also buy loose stones, especially opals; the high-quality Australian varieties are recognized as some of the best in the world. You can purchase such stones and jewelry tax free. The value of an opal is judged by the depth of hue. Red is the most prized, followed by orange, yellow, green, blue, indigo and violet. Buy only solid opals, not inferior doublets or triplets. South Sea pearls are graded by luster, tone, size, shape, surface perfection and rarity.

Shopping by Theme

Whether you're looking for a shopping mall, a quirky market or a trendy boutique, you'll find it all in Sydney. On this page, shops are listed by theme. For a more detailed write-up, see the page listed.

ANTIQUES/CRAFTS

Berrima Village Pottery (▷ 104)
The Brook (▷ 104)

AUSTRALIANA

The ABC Shop (▷ 84)
Aboriginal Art Galleries (▷ 49)
The Australian Geographic Shop (▷ 104)
Craft NSW (▷ 49)
Ken Duncan Gallery (▷ 49)
The Rocks Centre (▷ 50)

BOOKS

Berkelouw Paddington (▷ 84)
Dymocks (▷ 85)
Gleebooks (▷ 63)
Gleebooks (Kids) (▷ 63)

CLOTHING

Adrienne & The Misses Bonney (▷ 84)
Between the Flags (▷ 49)
Bondi Surf Co. (▷ 104)
Country Road (▷ 84)
Peter Sheppard (▷ 86)
Rip Curl Surf Shop (▷ 104)
R. M. Williams (▷ 86)
Strand Hatters (▷ 86)
Tuchuzy (▷ 104)

DEPARTMENT STORE

David Jones (▷ 85)

FOOD/WINE

The Australian Wine Centre (▷ 49)
Blue Mountains Chocolate Company (▷ 104)
David Jones Food Hall (▷ 85)
Just William Chocolates (▷ 85)
Paris Cake Shop (▷ 104)
The Nut Shop (▷ 86)
Thai-Kee Supermarket (▷ 63)

JEWELRY

Dinosaur Designs (▷ 85)
The Family Jewels (▷ 85)
Hardy Brothers (▷ 85)
Opal Fields (▷ 49)
Opal Minded (▷ 49)
Paspaley Pearls (▷ 86)

MARKETS

Balmain Market (▷ 63)
Bondi Markets (▷ 104)
EQ Village Markets (▷ 85)
Glebe Markets (▷ 63)
Paddington Markets (▷ 86)
Paddy's Markets (▷ 63)
The Rocks Market (▷ 50)
Sydney Fish Market (▷ 62)

MUSIC

Birdland Records (▷ 84)

SHOPPING AREAS

Castlereagh Street (▷ 84)
Chinatown and Haymarket (▷ 63)
Double Bay (▷ 85)
The Rocks (▷ 49)

SHOPPING MALLS

Chifley Plaza (▷ 84)
Harbourside Darling Harbour (▷ 63)
MLC Centre (▷ 85)
Queen Victoria Building (▷ 86)
The Strand Arcade (▷ 86)
Sussex Centre (▷ 63)
Warringah Mall (▷ 104)

Sydney by Night

Restaurants offering alfresco dining, bars with spectacular views and nightclubs that stay open late keep Sydney lively after dark. A huge influx of immigrants in the last few years has energized the restaurant scene as well.

The Music Scene and More

The area from Circular Quay (▷ 46) around to the Sydney Opera House (▷ 30–31) bustles at night; Newtown, Darlinghurst and Paddington have the hippest nightclubs, pubs and bars; and Surry Hills and Balmain have several pubs where you can catch the sounds of jazz, rock and blues bands.

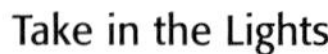

Take in the Lights

Take the elevator to the observation deck of Sydney Tower (▷ 78; last entry summer 9pm, winter 8.30pm) for a glittering panorama of Sydney Harbour (▷ 26) and the city, or take a meal in one of the revolving restaurants. Even when the tower is closed, it's worth your while to take in the views from the adjoining park. Walk down the hill for dinner in North Beach or Chinatown (▷ 56–57).

Drink with a View

Bright lights and fabulous views—Sydney by night

Relax with a cocktail as you take in the view from the 36th floor in the Shangri-la Hotel (▷ 112). Or head for the ECQ Bar above Circular Quay at the Pullman Quay Grand Sydney Harbour (✉ 61 Macquarie Street). It is listed as one of the world's best bars and serves great *tapas*. When hunger strikes, consider Quay (▷ 52) on the Upper Level of the Overseas Passenger Terminal, one of Sydney's finest restaurants.

ON THE WATER AND DANCING

Take a night cruise of Sydney Harbour aboard the *John Cadman*. Captain Cook Cruises (☎ 9206 1122) offer a three-course à la carte menu to enjoy as you pass well-known city landmarks. The tour includes entertainment and dancing.

Eating Out

Sydney is such a multicultural city that it's not surprising to find food from all corners of the globe within a radius of a few miles. Food courts of shopping malls are often a tempting aggregation of the world's cuisines.

What's on the Menu?

Sydney, one of the world's culinary capitals, is home to chefs who have made a worldwide reputation. Modern Australian cuisine, which fuses European and Asian food styles with local ingredients, has arrived as a distinct cutting-edge cuisine. In recent years, dishes incorporating Aboriginal foods containing bush tucker ingredients, such as kangaroo, emu, crocodile and native fruits and nuts, have been added to the menu. Asian restaurants are everywhere, including world-class Chinese, along with refined cuisine from Indonesia, India, Taiwan, Korea and Vietnam. The fruits of the sea play a large role in Sydney menus and local specialties include Sydney rock oysters, kingfish, enormous prawns, scallops and squid. Appropriately, many seafood restaurants have waterfront locations, where you can buy excellent fish-and-chips to take out—Bondi Beach (▷ 94), Circular Quay (▷ 46) and Manly (▷ 95) are particularly good spots for alfresco dining.

Sydney's Budget Resturants

Many restaurants are reasonably priced and are BYO (bring your own alcohol). Apart from the many food courts, good areas offering budget meals include Oxford Street, Paddington, King Street, Newtown, Glebe Point Road, Glebe, Chinatown at Haymarket, Darling Harbour (▷ 60–61) and Circular Quay (▷ 46).

WINES OF NEW SOUTH WALES

Hunter Valley wines, exported to Europe, the US and Asia, are worth seeking out. There are many varieties to go with your food, including Cabernet Sauvignon, Shiraz, Chardonnay and Semillon. Good winemakers to look for include McWilliam's, Rosemont, Rothbury Estate and Tyrell's.

The pick of the ocean in Sydney's beachside restaurants

Restaurants by Cuisine

There are restaurants to suit all tastes and budgets in Sydney. On this page, they are listed by cuisine. For a more detailed description of each restaurant, see the page listed.

AUSTRALIAN

Aria (▷ 52)
Ashcrofts (▷ 106)
Bistro Moncur (▷ 89)
Cafe Sydney (▷ 51)
Civic Bistro (▷ 89)
Cruise Bar (▷ 51)
Dunbar House (▷ 106)
Est (▷ 51)
Hicksons Food & Wine (▷ 51)
MCA Café (▷ 51)
Mos Café (▷ 51)
Pavilion on the Park (▷ 90)
Q Dining (▷ 52)
Quarryman's Hotel (▷ 66)
Riverbend Restaurant (▷ 106)
Sydney Tower 360 (▷ 90)

CAFÉS

Bar Coluzzi (▷ 89)
Bills (▷ 89)
Caffe Otto (▷ 66)
Gusto (▷ 89)
Hyde Park Barracks Café (▷ 90)

CHINESE

Chinatown Centre (▷ 66)
Fisherman's Wharf (▷ 66)
Golden Century (▷ 66)
The Malaya (▷ 66)
Mr Wong (▷ 52)
Neptune Palace (▷ 52)

INDIAN

Flavour of India (▷ 89)

ITALIAN

Bondi Trattoria (▷ 106)
Icebergs Dining Room (▷ 106)
Lucio's (▷ 90)

JAPANESE

Catalina (▷ 106)
Ippudo (▷ 90)
Sokyo (▷ 66)
Tetsuya's (▷ 90)

MEXICAN

Pepino's (▷ 66)

MODERN MED

Bathers Pavilion Restaurant (▷ 36)
Capitan Torres (▷ 89)
Sean's Panaroma (▷ 106)

OTHER EUROPEAN

Baroque (▷ 51)
Bistro CBD (▷ 89)
Globe Bar & Brasserie (▷ 51)
Lowenbrau Keller (▷ 51)
Quay Bar (▷ 52)
Sir Stamford at Circular Quay (▷ 52)

SEAFOOD

Balkan Seafood (▷ 89)
Doyles on the Beach (▷ 106)
Longrain (▷ 90)
Quay (▷ 52)
Rockpool (▷ 52)
Sydney Cove Oyster Bar (▷ 36)
Watsons Beach Club (▷ 36)

THAI/VIETNAMESE

Sailors Thai (▷ 52)
Thai Prasert (▷ 36)
Tum Tum's Thai Takeaway (▷ 90)

VEGETARIAN

Sappho Books Cafe & Wine Bar (▷ 66)

Note: The use of the accent on the word "café" is not universally used in Australian English.

Top Tips For...

However you'd like to spend your time in Sydney, these top suggestions should help you tailor your ideal visit. Each site or listing has a fuller write-up in Sydney by Area.

SAMPLING LOCAL CUISINE

Sample the Chinese cuisine at Mr Wong (▷ 52), a Sydneysider favorite for its Cantonese food and colonial decor.

Sydney's best seafood cuisine can be enjoyed in stylish surroundings at Rockpool (▷ 52) in a heritage building on Bridge Street.

Pretty as a picture—seafood on a plate and alfresco dining (above)

OUTDOOR DINING

Boasting stunning ocean vistas, Icebergs Dining Room (▷ 106) at Bondi serves tasty Mediterranean fare in a great setting.

Sit outoors at Doyles on the Beach (▷ 106) at Watsons Bay and enjoy waterside views with the CBD in the distance.

BUDGET CLOTHING

Paddy's Markets (▷ 63) sells quality brand clothing as well as men's and women's underwear and lingerie.

Head for Paddington Markets (▷ 86) in Oxford Street on Saturday, for original designs, alternative fashions and casual wear.

FREE THINGS

At the Royal Botanic Gardens (▷ 24–25) you can stroll among a great plant collection in a superb setting.

See some of Australia's most admired paintings, sculptures and decorative arts at the Art Gallery of New South Wales (▷ 72).

Get down to the market (above right) or soak up some culture at the Art Gallery of NSW (right)

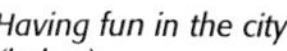

Having fun in the city (below)

LEARNING ABOUT LOCAL CULTURE

An excellent collection of decorative arts, including many utilitarian objects from the past, can be viewed at the Powerhouse Museum (⊳ 59) at Pyrmont.

The Australian Museum (⊳ 70–71) has one of the world's best collections of Aboriginal cultural objects in its permanent exhibition.

GOING OUT ON THE TOWN

Dress up and make your way to Blu Bar on 36 (⊳ 50) where the cocktails are served with a stunning Harbour backdrop.

If you feel like a flutter, The Star (⊳ 62) offers slot machines, blackjack, roulette and a host of other games of chance, but remember to dress up smart.

Take at break at Bondi (above)

STAYING AT BUDGET HOTELS

At Y on the Park (⊳ 109) there are comfortable single and double en suite rooms and great facilities.

Stay at the beachside at Bondi Beachouse YHA (⊳ 109) with good basic accommodations including double rooms with private bathrooms.

ENTERTAINING THE KIDS

At City Farm (⊳ 105) adults can have as much fun as kids interacting with the many farm animals on display.

The Powerhouse Museum (⊳ 59) has lots of things to see and hands-on exhibits that keep young ones—and some of the old ones, too—entertained.

Sydney Wild Life Zoo (⊳ 62) has creatures galore to fascinate children.

Angora lambs down at the farm (left)

Have a night on the tiles or take a trip to the country

A GIRLS' NIGHT OUT

One of Sydney's most popular pubs, the Mercantile Hotel (▷ 50) at The Rocks, has live music most nights.

At Cherry (▷ 64), at The Star in Pyrmont, you can sip cocktails and hear house, disco and Balearic beat.

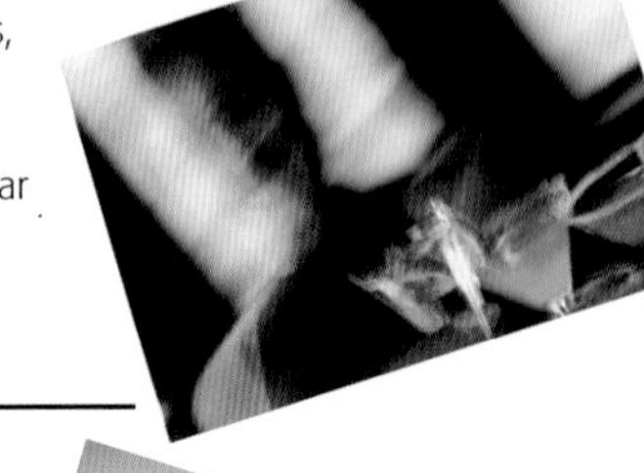

A WALK ON THE WILD SIDE

Sydney Harbour National Park (▷ 28–29) has lots of walking trails where you can discover original native vegetation.

The scenic Blue Mountains (▷ 102), just over an hour's drive from the CBD, has many forest walking trails. Its towns boast excellent hotels, restaurants and quaint shops.

CUTTING-EDGE ARCHITECTURE

One of the world's most dramatic buildings, the Sydney Opera House (▷ 30–31) has a tour that reveals its design history.

Chifley Tower (▷ 79) has a unique shape and an excellent shopping mall that includes a food court.

Close-up of the iconic Sydney Opera House

BIRDS AND ANIMALS

Check out one of Australia's top wildlife parks, Koala Park Sanctuary (▷ 100), set in the forest at West Pennant Hills.

Home to the full range of Australia's wildife—including platypus, echidna, kangaroo and koala—Taronga Zoo (▷ 32–33) also has a dramatic setting on the water's edge.

Look carefully and you might spy a joey in the koala's pouch (right)

SUPPLY
Sydney Ferries
SUPPLY

Sydney Harbour and North Sydney

The magnificent and iconic Harbour, around which Sydney has developed, is both a transport route and a recreational domain from where you'll see the city at its finest.

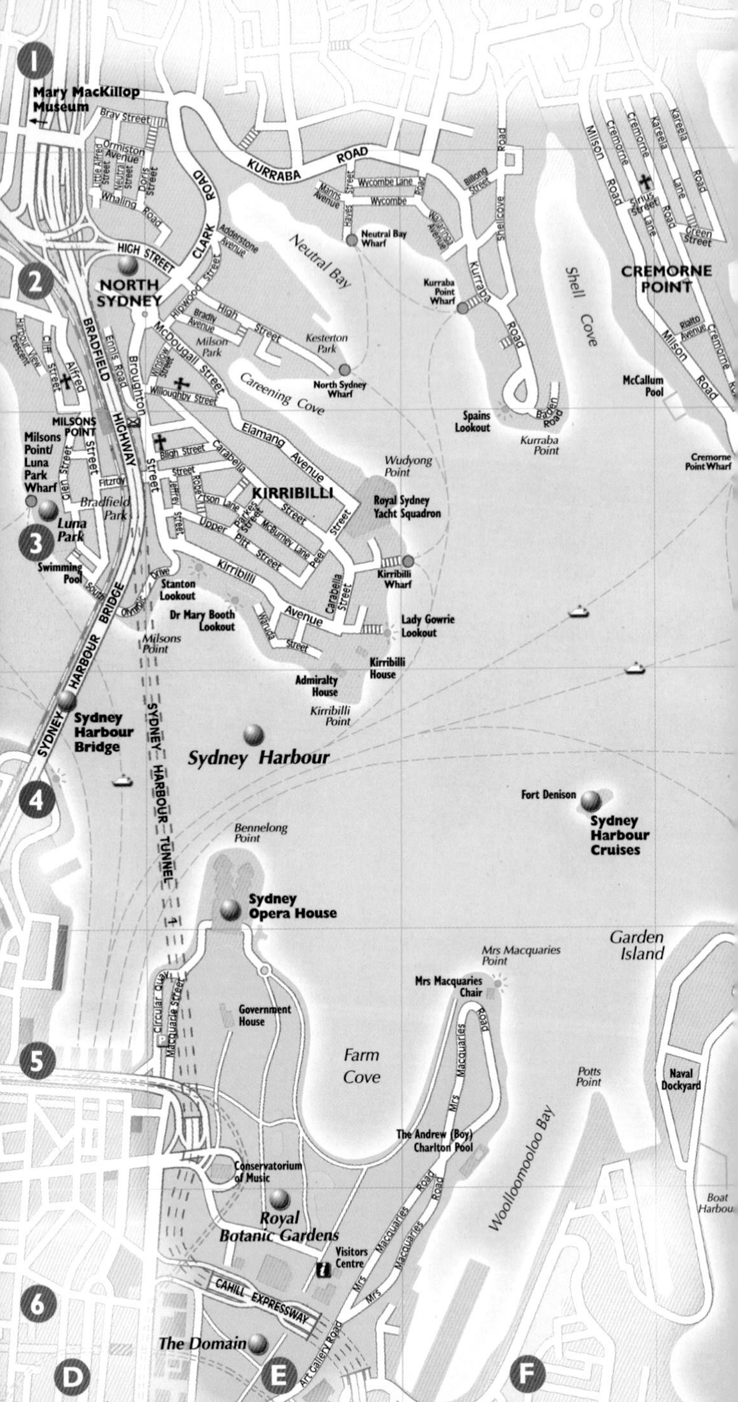

Mary MacKillop Museum
North Sydney
Kirribilli
Milsons Point
Luna Park
Cremorne Point
Neutral Bay
Careening Cove
Shell Cove
Sydney Harbour Bridge
Sydney Harbour
Sydney Harbour Tunnel
Fort Denison
Sydney Harbour Cruises
Sydney Opera House
Garden Island
Mrs Macquaries Chair
Farm Cove
Woolloomooloo Bay
Potts Point
Naval Dockyard
Royal Botanic Gardens
Government House
Conservatorium of Music
Visitors Centre
The Domain
Cahill Expressway
Kirribilli House
Admiralty House
Royal Sydney Yacht Squadron

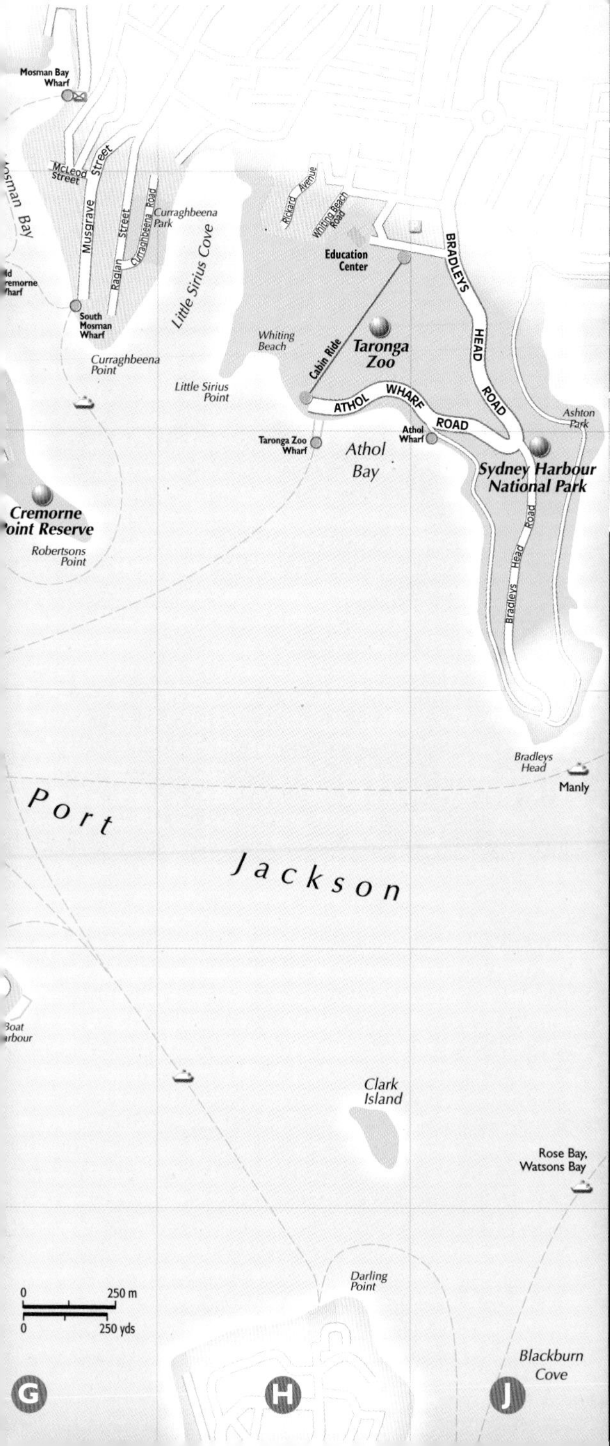

Mosman Bay Wharf
McLeod Street
Musgrave Street
Raglan Street
Curraghbeena Road
Curraghbeena Park
Mosman Bay
Little Sirius Cove
South Mosman Wharf
Curraghbeena Point
Little Sirius Point
Rickard Avenue
Whiting Beach Road
Education Center
Whiting Beach
Cabin Ride
Taronga Zoo
BRADLEYS HEAD ROAD
ATHOL WHARF ROAD
Taronga Zoo Wharf
Athol Wharf
Athol Bay
Ashton Park
Sydney Harbour National Park
Bradleys Head Road
Cremorne Point Reserve
Robertsons Point
Bradleys Head
Manly
Port Jackson
Clark Island
Rose Bay, Watsons Bay
Darling Point
Blackburn Cove
0 250 m
0 250 yds
G H J

Royal Botanic Gardens and the Domain

TOP 25

HIGHLIGHTS

- Sydney Tropical Centre
- Sydney Fernery
- Palm Grove
- Herb Garden
- Visitor Centre
- Gardens Shop
- Free guided walks
- Government House
- Walk around Farm Cove to Mrs Macquaries Point
- Views from Mrs Macquaries Point
- Scenic train tour by Choo-Choo Express

To escape the crowds of central Sydney, visit the glorious Botanic Gardens, once an Aboriginal sacred site, then take a stroll in the Domain, a waterside haven for kookaburras and cockatoos.

Royal Botanic Gardens Extending inland from the Farm Cove, these lovely gardens were the site of the first government farm back in 1788. The gardens were founded in 1816 and now contain a fine collection of native and foreign plants. The highlights include the Sydney Fernery and the Sydney Tropical Centre with its modern glass-houses. Here the wonders of tropical ecosystems are explained and there is a display of plants from around the world. You can also wander through the delightful Palm Grove, or visit the beautifully laid-out Herb Garden, the Visitor Centre and Gardens Shop

Clockwise from far left: the main pond at the Royal Botanic Gardens; trees in the park; flower beds and palms by the Pyramid at the gardens' tropical house; a white sulphur-crested cockatoo in the Domain; Government House in the Domain

and the National Herbarium, established in 1985 to study Australia's native plants. The impressive Government House, once the official residence of the governor of New South Wales, lies within the gardens and is open to the public.

The Domain The northern section of the Domain (the remainder fronts the Art Gallery of NSW on the other side of the Cahill Expressway and is used mainly by lunchtime joggers and for open-air concerts in summer) is part of the land laid out in 1810 as the "domain" of Governor Macquarie. This tree-lined area is a lovely spot for picnics and water-front strolls. In summer, you can have a dip at the open-air Andrew "Boy" Charlton swimming pool and walk to Mrs Macquaries Point, named after the governor's wife who, not surprisingly, enjoyed the wonderful view from this promontory.

THE BASICS

www.rbgsyd.nsw.gov.au

E6

Mrs Macquaries Road

Botanic Gardens 9231 8111. Government House infoline 9228 4111

Gardens daily 7am–dusk. Glasshouses daily 10–4; closed Good Fri, 25 Dec. Government House Fri–Sun 10.30–3

Botanic Gardens Restaurant 12–2.30. Botanic Gardens Café 8.30–4.30. Pavilion kiosk 7.30–4

Circular Quay/Martin Place

200, 441

Circular Quay

Very good

Free

Sydney Harbour

A striking contrast of views over Sydney Harbour

THE BASICS

www.shfa.nsw.gov.au
E4
Fort Denison, Sydney Harbour
9240 8500
Tours daily of Circular Quay and The Rocks
Circular Quay
Free shuttle or alll buses bound for Circular Quay
From Circular Quay

HIGHLIGHTS

- Ferry ride or cruise
- Fort Denison
- Views from South Head and North Head
- Goat Island
- The Spit to Manly Walk (▷ 101)
- Picnic on Shark Island

TIP

- Choose your day carefully for a boat trip if you are prone to sea sickness.

Spectacular Sydney Harbour, officially Port Jackson, undoubtedly makes this city special. You get stunning water views from the most unexpected places and the still waters are a wonderful place for sailing. Be sure to take a ferry ride to Manly.

Sydney Harbour With a shoreline that stretches for 240km (149 miles), Sydney Harbour is guaranteed to delight. The best way to enjoy this setting is to take a ferry ride or cruise, most of which depart from Circular Quay—you can even travel on an elegant square-rigged schooner. You can visit beautiful Cremorne Point, Taronga Zoo (▷ 32–33), Manly (▷ 95) and Watsons Bay (▷ 101), or take an evening cruise to view the city lights. Harborside walks, such as those around North Head or South Head, are also popular, while Sydney Harbour National Park (▷ 28–29) encompasses Shark, Clark, Goat and Rodd islands, which can be toured. After you have taken in the obvious attractions of the main part of the Harbour, head west beyond the Harbour Bridge or take a RiverCat trip upriver to Parramatta or Homebush Bay, or travel by ferry to the suburbs of Balmain, Birchgrove, Greenwich, Hunters Hill and Meadowbank.

Fort Denison This island was once known as "Pinchgut", after the practise of marooning disobedient convicts here with extremely meager rations. By 1857 the island had become Fort Denison, built to defend Sydney against possible Russian invasion during the Crimean War.

An iconic view of Sydney Harbour Bridge and the Opera House in the late evening

TOP 25 Sydney Harbour Bridge

Affectionately called "the coat hanger" by locals, the Sydney Harbour Bridge is one of the most famous symbols of this city. Take a climb to the top of the bridge for great views, an energetic climb that's not for the fainthearted.

All things to all people This bridge is an essential link between the south and north sides of the Harbour, the perfect postcard backdrop to the Opera House, and a great spot to take in the panorama. The world's widest long-span bridge was opened in March 1932. The arch spans 503m (1650ft) and the bridge carries eight road lanes, two railway tracks, a cycleway and a footpath. Crossing by car, bus or train just isn't the same—the best experience is walking across. From the city side, access to the walkway is via Argyle Street in The Rocks, while the northern entrance is near Milsons Point station; a ferry service operates between Milsons Point and Circular Quay.

Take in the view The highlight of a walk across the bridge is a stop at the southeast pylon. There is an interesting display here on how the bridge was constructed, and the 200-step climb to the lookout is well worthwhile, for the views of the Harbour and the city are magnificent.

BridgeClimb For a bird's-eye view of the city and surrounds you can take the three-hour climb to the top of the bridge's arch. Professional guides accompany you on day and night climbs with strict safety measures in place.

THE BASICS

www.sydney.com.au/bridge.html

D4

9240 1100, www.pylonlookout.com.au; 8274 7777 www.bridgeclimb.com

Lookout daily 10–5; closed 25 Dec

Circular Quay (southern side)

Sydney Explorer

Milsons Point (northern side)

Circular Quay (southern side)

Walkway free. Pylon Lookout moderate. BridgeClimb expensive

HIGHLIGHTS

- The walk across
- View from the Pylon Lookout
- Pylon Lookout display
- Close-up look at the structure
- A climb to the top of the bridge

Sydney Harbour National Park

HIGHLIGHTS

- Fort Denison
- Shark Island
- Quarantine Station
- Nielsen Park
- Middle Head forts

TIP

- Be sure to pack a hat, sunscreen and protective clothing for the ferry journeys.

There is no better way to get to know the many stunning bays and inlets and their surrounding suburbs than by exploring the multisectioned Sydney Harbour National Park.

Early days The park contains remnants of bushland common before white settlement and many cultural and heritage attractions. You can visit convict-built buildings, historic maritime and military installations and recreational islands. The Quarantine Station (▷ 100) at North Head, which isolated new arrivals with infectious diseases from Sydneysiders, has nighttime ghost walks. At Middle Head are the remains of a network of forts that were built around the Harbour for protection from, among others, the Russians in the 19th century and the Japanese in the 1940s.

Clockwise from far left: a view across the water from Bradleys Head; stained-glass window at Watson's Chapel at South Head in the National Park; plenty of space in the park; Sydney skyline with Clark Island in the mid-distance; kookaburra in the park; a view of Sydney Harbour

Other park highlights Ferry tours ply to the tiny colonial penal relic Fort Denison, Australia's only Martello Tower. Here an audiovisual presentation highlights its history, including its time as a high-security prison. Enjoy a relaxing ferry trip to tiny Shark Island, spectacularly set in the middle of Sydney Harbour. This is the perfect place for a picnic, with its trees and picnic shelters—there is even a small beach where you can enjoy a swim. There are many walks, including the Manly Scenic Walkway, with its native coastal heath and subtropical rainforest remnants. On the south side of the Harbour, the 1.5km (1 mile), easy Hermitage Foreshore Track starts in Nielsen Park at Vaucluse and takes you through a strip of protected bushland, winding along the western edge of Vaucluse and finishing at Bayview Hill Road. A swim at Nielsen Park beach is a treat.

THE BASICS

www.nationalparks.nsw.gov.au

J3

Information: Cadman's Cottage, George Street, The Rocks

9247 5033 (and for ferry bookings)

Fort Denison tours run daily from Cadman's Cottage. Shark Island ferries run from Darling Harbour and Circular Quay

Moderate

Sydney Opera House

TOP 25

HIGHLIGHTS

- Bennelong Point
- Ceramic-tiled roof
- Concert Hall
- Opera Theatre
- *Five Bells* mural by Australian artist John Olsen
- *Possum Dreaming* mural by Michael Tjakamarra

TIP

- Be sure to book for the two-hour backstage tour.

This once controversial, yet ethereal, sail-roofed building rising from the water on its prominent bayside site epitomizes the free-spirited nature of this young and vibrant city.

Sydney's most recognizable building The Opera House was conceived by Danish architect Jørn Utzon, who won a design competition in 1959. It took 14 years to create this masterpiece, which was opened in 1973 by Queen Elizabeth II, although the project was fraught with technical and political problems and Utzon eventually resigned. The building holds six performance halls—for plays, dance, symphony concerts, opera and other events—restaurants and bars, and a maze of backstage areas. The open-air forecourt turns the Harbour into a

Clockwise from far left: people abseiling on the roof of Sydney Opera House; interior of the magnificent concert hall; take a ferry past the famous building; rooftop closeup; detail of a rooftop "sail"; crowds come out to view the Harbour on Australia Day

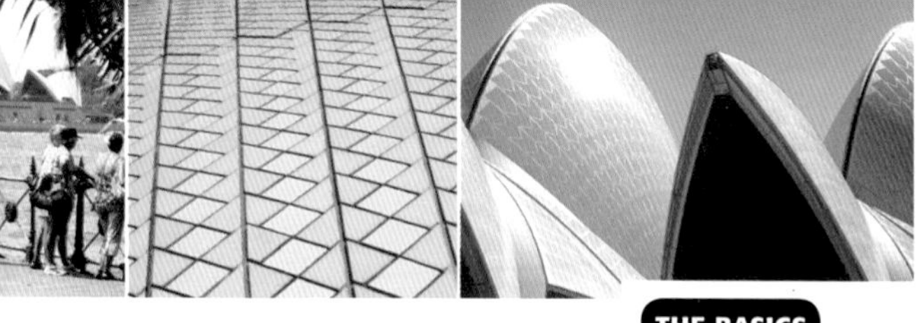

stage. The roofs are covered with more than a million ceramic tiles, and the stone base and terraces are fashioned on the Mayan and Aztec temples of Mexico. You can enjoy the exterior at any time; a walk around gives you a chance to view the building from many perspectives.

The interior While the architect's vision for the interior was never fully realized, there is much to see here including a John Olsen mural, *Salute to Five Bells*, in the northern foyer of the Concert Hall, and a Michael Tjakamarra mural, titled *Possum Dreaming*, in the foyer of the Opera Theatre. Take a walk around the building for a different perspective of the CBD and the Harbour Bridge. If possible, attend a performance or take a guided tour to fully appreciate this world-famous icon.

THE BASICS

www.sydneyoperahouse.com

E4

Bennelong Point

Tours 9250 7250; box office 9250 7777

Tours daily 7–5. Performances most days. Closed Good Fri, 25 Dec

Four restaurants and cafés also theater bars

Circular Quay

Any Circular Quay bus

Circular Quay

Good

Tours: expensive

Taronga Zoo

TOP 25

Australia's best-loved koalas meet Africa's splendid giraffes

THE BASICS

www.taronga.org.au
H2
Bradleys Head Road, Mosman
9969 2777
Daily Sep–Apr 9–5; May–Aug 9.30–4.30
The View restaurant, cafés and picnic areas
247
Taronga Zoo
Good
Expensive

HIGHLIGHTS

- Western Lowland gorillas
- Australian Walkabout
- Snow leopards
- Seal shows
- "Orang-utan Walk"
- White Sumatran tiger
- Platypus and echidna
- Views from the cable car
- Koala bears
- Rainforest Aviary

TIP

- Arrive by ferry and take the Ski Safari up to the top.

Located in Sydney Harbour, Taronga Zoo is a conservation leader. Although it doesn't limit itself to native animals, its Australian animals are most popular. The ferry ride to get there is a bonus.

Australian wildlife Set in natural foreshore bushland, Taronga (an Aboriginal word meaning water view) dates from 1916 and has long been at the forefront of keeping animals in less restrictive enclosures. This is a great place to see emus, kangaroos, wallabies, dingoes, wombats, the carnivorous Tasmanian devil, crocodiles and many native birds. As always, the koalas are a must-see, particularly as you can have your photo taken next to one of these endearing creatures. Don't miss the echidna and the aquatic platypus (examples of monotremes—egg-laying mammals). Other highlights include seal and bird shows, the Orang-utan Walk, Lemur Forest Adventure, African Safari and Giraffe Encounter, and the komodo dragons that inhabit the Reptile World. Taronga has an educational bias and a variety of animal presentations and keeper talks take place each day. Guided zoo tours include a peek into the wildlife hospital.

Creatures from other countries Taronga's strong support for wildlife conservation is evident in its endangered species breeding agenda; the zoo is home to Sumatran tigers, Himalayan snow leopards, red pandas, Western Lowland gorillas, black rhinoceros, Asian elephants, Fijian crested iguanas and chimpanzees.

Sydney's
TARONGA ZOO

More to See

CREMORNE POINT RESERVE

www.northsydney.nsw.gov.au

A walk at this reserve reveals a portion of the city that visitors seldom see. From the wharf, turn left and walk along the reserve's western section, which gives fine views of the city. Walk up the steps opposite the wharf and head to the left, where you can stroll around the waterside, past lush gardens and homes with outlooks to tranquil Mosman Bay. From here, the ferry will take you to Circular Quay.

G3 Cremorne 9936 8100 Daily Free

LUNA PARK

www.lunaparksydney.com

This restored 1930s amusement park, set on the Harbour foreshores, has crazy rides including a roller coaster, games and extra seasonal attractions for kids during school holidays.

D3 Olympic Drive, Milsons Point 9922 6644 Daily hours vary; check website for operational rides Bar and food outlets Milsons Point Milsons Point Expensive

MARY MACKILLOP MUSEUM

www.marymackillopplace.org.au

Beatified in 1995, Mary MacKillop championed the poor in Australia. State-of-the-art electronics, animatronics and theatrics show Mary's life.

Off map at C1 Mary MacKillop Place, 7 Mount Street, North Sydney 8912 4878 Daily 10–4; closed 25 Dec Coffee shop North Sydney Moderate

NORTH SYDNEY

www.taronga.org.au

The suburb of North Sydney has a collection of office buildings and retail outlets that border the Harbour.

D2 North Sydney Many cafés and restaurants North Sydney (from CBD) 261, 263

SYDNEY HARBOUR CRUISES

www.sydneyharbourcruises.com.au

Learn about the Harbour, its bays and waterways on a variety of cruises.

F4 Captain Cook Cruises, No. 6 Jetty, Circular Quay 9206 1122 Daily from 9.30am Coffee and dinner cruises Circular Quay Moderate

The face of Luna Park

A cruise around Sydney Harbour

Taronga Zoo to Balmoral Beach

This interesting Harbour walk runs along the northern foreshores and features spectacular views, historic sights and natural bushland.

DISTANCE: 6km (4 miles) **ALLOW**: 3 hours

START

TARONGA ZOO FERRY TERMINAL
H2 Taronga Zoo ferry

❶ From the ferry terminal head east, and after 300m (330 yards) there is a walking track to the right. Follow this along the water's edge to Bradley's Head, offering great views.

❷ Continue on, taking short sidetracks if you have time. Near Bradley's Head is Athol, which has a café. The walk now follows a wooden walking platform on the east side.

❸ The walkway becomes a bush track that runs north and you can see the Harbour. In about 300m (330 yards) you reach the southern end of Taylor's Bay.

❹ From Taylor's Bay the track heads off into bushland behind the beach, then turns north to reach a small headland. Take a short detour to the lookout before continuing.

❺ Walk 300m (330 yards) to the beach at Clifton Gardens for a swim.

❻ After a rest look for the gate at the northern end of the beach (locked from dusk to dawn) and walk up the steps to the roundabout at the road. Here you will see a sign-posted track to West Head Road.

❼ The roads runs for 1.5km (1 mile) through old army land. Check out the old forts and buildings. Contine over West Head Road, and follow a track leading you to a set of stairs. Follow the track down to the oval at the bottom, then head toward the Harbour.

❽ Take the left turn and walk up the beach to Balmoral Village. From here you can take a bus to Neutral Bay and ferry back to Circular Quay.

BALMORAL BEACH
G9 257 to Neutral Bay, then ferry

END

Entertainment and Nightlife

NORTH SYDNEY OLYMPIC POOL

This harborside pool, with lovely views, is open-air in summer, but covered by a "bubble" in cooler months. Spa and sauna upstairs.
D3 4 Alfred Street South, Milsons Point 9955 2309 Mon–Fri 5.30am–9pm, Sat–Sun 7–7 Milsons Point

OZ JET BOATING

www.ozjetboating.com
Explore Sydney Harbour at speed by jet boat. See the sights and experience the thrills of jet spins, slides, fishtails and powerbrake stops.
D5 Circular Quay's Eastern Pontoon 1300 556 111 Daily summer 11–5, winter 11–4 Circular Quay Circular Quay

WHALE WATCHING

www.sydneywhalewatching.com
Commentaries on whales and Harbour sights. Departures from Darling Harbour, Circular Quay and Manly.
C6 Wharf 8, King Street, Darling Harbour 1800 309 672 Mid-May to early Dec, 4-hour and 2.5-hour cruises Town Hall

Restaurants

PRICES

Prices are approximate, based on a 3-course meal for one person.
$$$ over A$60
$$ A$40–A$60
$ under A$40

BATHERS PAVILION RESTAURANT ($$$)

www.batherspavilion.com.au
Lush interior with views over the beach. Offers modern European-style, particularly French, dishes with the emphasis on fresh produce. There's a more casual café, too.
J2 4 The Esplanade, Balmoral Beach 9969 5050 Daily lunch, dinner

SYDNEY COVE OYSTER BAR ($$–$$$)

www.sydneycoveoysterbar.com
Here you'll find light and tasty seafood and superlative oysters in a stunning Harbour setting near the Opera House. Enjoy panoramic waterside views from the outdoor seating.
E5 1 Circular Quay East 9247 2937 Daily snacks, lunch and dinner Circular Quay

FOOD AFLOAT

There is no better way to experience the Harbour's magic than by dining on the water. Although the cuisine of these floating restaurants rarely reaches gourmet standards, lunch or dinner cruises are understandably popular. Operators include Captain Cook Cruises (lunches and dinners 9206 1111), Matilda Cruises (lunches and dinners 8270 5188) and Sydney Ferries offer morning, afternoon and evening cruises with onboard food and expert commentary.

THAI PRASERT ($$)

www.thaiprasert.com.au
Rich green, yellow, duck and vegetarian curries are some of the tasty specialties of this sophisticated Thai restaurant.
D1 77 Mount Street, North Sydney 9957 2271 Mon–Fri lunch, dinner North Sydney

WATSONS BEACH CLUB ($$–$$$)

www.watsonsbayhotel.com.au
Very popular because of its location, the Beach Club serves all-day breakfasts (including vegetarian), salads, burgers and plenty of seafood.
J6 Watsons Bay Hotel 9337 5444 Daily lunch 324, 325 Watsons Bay

Circular Quay and The Rocks

This waterside precinct, the historic core of Sydney, has fine views of the Harbour Bridge and Opera House, and is accessible on foot. The Rocks has some of the best restored buildings in the city.

3
Drummoyne, Woolwich
Goat Island
Thames Street Wharf
4
Walsh Bay
Millers Point
Dawes Point
Pier One
DAWES POINT
Wharf Theatre
Hickson Road
Hickson Road
Pottinger Street
Fort Street
Lower Fort
BRADFIELD HIGHWAY
Towns Place
Dalgety Road
Merriman Street
Windmill Street
Trinity Avenue
THE ROCKS
Argyle Place
Argyle Street
Watson Road
Playfair Street
Sydney Observatory
Upper Fort Street
Toll Gates
Cumberland Street
MILLERS POINT
Kent Street
Hickson Road
Museum of Contemporary Art
CAHILL EXPRESSWAY
Alfred
5
Johnstons Bay
Gloucester
Harrington
George
Grosvenor Place
Pitt Street
Dalley Street
Maritime Centre
WESTERN DISTRIBUTOR
GROSVENOR STREET
Bridge
Pitt Street
6
7
0 250 m
0 250 yds
B
C
D

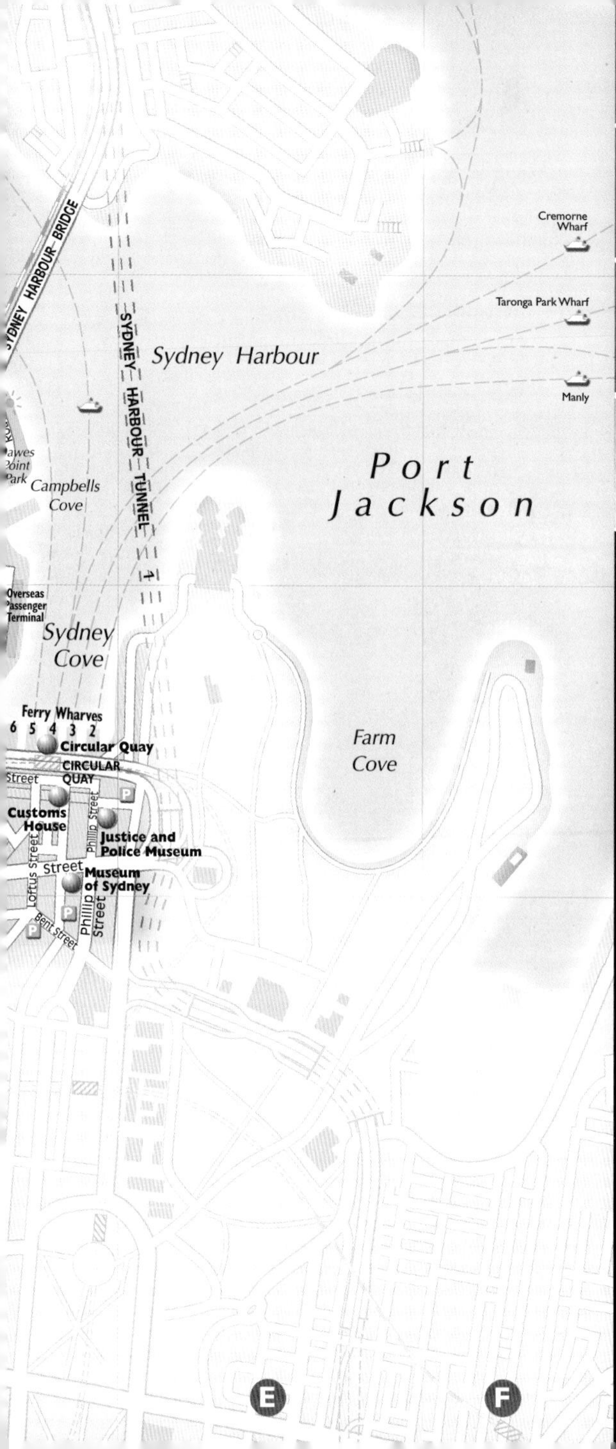

SYDNEY HARBOUR BRIDGE
SYDNEY HARBOUR TUNNEL
Sydney Harbour
Cremorne Wharf
Taronga Park Wharf
Manly
Port Jackson
Dawes Point Park
Campbells Cove
Overseas Passenger Terminal
Sydney Cove
Ferry Wharves
6 5 4 3 2
Circular Quay
CIRCULAR QUAY
Street
Customs House
Phillip Street
Justice and Police Museum
Loftus Street
Street
Museum of Sydney
Bent Street
Phillip Street
Farm Cove
1
E
F

Museum of Contemporary Art

HIGHLIGHTS

- Art deco building
- Visiting exhibitions
- Indigenous art
- Free guided tours
- MCA shop and café

TIP

- Wheelchairs can be borrowed from the information desk at no charge.

The MCA is a modern art gallery full of surprises. Stunning installations, audacious photography, fine Aboriginal art and special performances all combine to astound and entertain.

The museum In a superb location overlooking the Harbour, the MCA contains Australia's finest collection of contemporary art. Established in 1991 by the University of Sydney, through a bequest of John Wardell Power and the provision of the building by the state government, the MCA contains more than 4,000 works. International visiting exhibitions, ranging from photography to 3D installations, are a well-worth seeing highlight and often occupy a large part of the gallery space, sending much of the permanent collection into temporary storage.

Clockwise from far left: photographic display at the Museum of Contemporary Art; puppy installation by Jeff Koons seen outside the museum during the Festival of Sydney; the museum's attractive waterside location; displays of modern art and installations

The permanent collection The Australian and international art exhibits date from the 1960s and include indigenous art from the Northern Territory's Arnhem Land, the Contemporary Art Archive and work by overseas artists such as Andy Warhol and Roy Lichtenstein.

The building This old building was once home to the Maritime Services Board. The structure was designed in 1939 but was not completed until 1954 due to the war and shortages of building materials. This makes it the last art deco style building in Sydney. Both the MCA Restaurant and the MCA Café offer magnificent views of the Opera House, and you'll find jewelry, bags, greeting cards, and an excellent range of books covering all aspects of contemporary art in the MCA Store.

THE BASICS

www.mca.com.au

D5

140 George Street, The Rocks

9245 2458

Daily 10–5, Thu 10–9; closed 25 Dec

Restaurant, café

Circular Quay

431, 432, 433

Circular Quay

Excellent Free

Free guided tours Mon–Wed and Fri 11 and 1, Thu 11, 1 and 7pm, Sat–Sun 11, 1 and 3. Special films, talks and performances

Museum of Sydney

TOP 25

The slick, modern building houses a treasure trove of the city's historic objects

THE BASICS

www.sydneylivingmuseums.com.au
D5
Corner of Bridge and Phillip streets
9251 5988
Daily 10–5; closed Good Fri, 25 Dec
Restaurant
Circular Quay
Any Circular Quay-bound bus
Circular Quay
Excellent
Moderate

HIGHLIGHTS

- *Edge of the Trees* sculpture and the public square
- Original Government House foundations
- Video wall
- State-of-the-art installations
- First Fleet model ships
- Changing exhibitions

This unusual museum leads you on a journey of discovery from the local Aboriginal occupation and the convict days of the late 18th century to the emerging Sydney of the 1850s and beyond.

The site The location forms an integral part of this exciting museum, for it was here that the nation's first, modest Government House was built in 1788. Home to the first nine governors, the building was demolished in 1846, but excavations have revealed the original foundations, part of which can be viewed through the paving. Emphasizing the nation's mixed origins, the dramatic forecourt sculpture, *Edge of the Trees*, consisting of 29 massive pillars of sandstone, wood and steeel, symbolizes the first Aboriginal encounter with the invading Europeans.

The museum Divided into several themed areas and laid out in an imaginative minimalist style, the three-level Museum of Sydney aims to interpret the city's past, present and future. Stories of the indigenous Cadigal people and the early European days are told through objects found during the excavations, computer displays, an extraordinary 33-screen video wall and spoken history.

Cadigal Place Gallery The exhibition in this one-room gallery tells the stories of individual indigenous Australians who had contact with the early settlers. Traditional cultural items are on display and you can watch a video of Aboriginal people talking about their lives and memories.

The Observatory, with its green domes, and the park are well away from the city bustle

TOP 25 Sydney Observatory

Sydney's glittering night skies are as intriguing today as they were for Australia's early astronomers, who built this fine building high on Observatory Hill in 1858.

The Observatory and Observatory Hill The Observatory, now a museum of astronomy and related sciences, provides a glimpse into those studies through hands-on exhibits and other displays. This is also the location for one of Sydney's most unusual tourist activities—night-sky viewing (reserved in advance). Observatory Hill is the city's highest point (44m/119ft) and was the site of Fort Phillip (1803), the original 1821 Observatory and the Signal Station (1848), which still stands today. There are great inner-Harbour views from the hill and you can walk behind the Observatory to visit the National Trust Centre, with its S. H. Ervin Gallery and excellent tearooms. The gallery features changing exhibitions of Australian art and culture, ranging from watercolor paintings to photography.

Argyle Place Just below Observatory Hill, and flanked by historic houses and the 1840 Gothic-revival Garrison Church, is Argyle Place. Also here is the sandstone Lord Nelson Hotel (1834), licensed since 1841. A stroll down nearby Lower Fort Street reveals more 19th-century terraced (row) houses and the charming, oddly shaped Hero of Waterloo Hotel (1843). From just above Argyle Place, you can walk, via the covered steps, on to the Sydney Harbour Bridge walkway.

THE BASICS

www.sydneyobservatory.com.au

C5

Watson Road, Observatory Hill, Millers Point

9921 3485

Daily 10–5 (late opening evenings according to season, check website for details). Closed Good Fri, 25 and 26 Dec

Café nearby

Circular Quay

431, 432, 433

Circular Quay

Few

Free; charge for night viewing (moderate)

9921 3485

HIGHLIGHTS

- Night tour with telescope viewing
- Hands-on scientific exhibits
- View from Observatory Hill
- 3-D Space Theatre
- S. H. Ervin Gallery
- Argyle Place
- Garrison Church

The Rocks

TOP 25

HIGHLIGHTS

- Campbells Cove
- Suez Canal and Nurses Walk
- The Rocks Market on weekends (▷ 50)
- Views from Dawes Point Park
- Local museums

TIP

- Take The Rocks walking tour, starting from the Visitor Centre.

The district known as The Rocks, Sydney's first "village", has a fascinating history as a colonial port area. Many of the restored old buildings now house interesting shops and galleries, restaurants and pubs.

A rocky start Named after the shore where convict tents were erected in January 1788, The Rocks is Sydney's most intriguing and picturesque area. It was once the province of seamen and traders, thieves and prostitutes, and the scene of a 1900 outbreak of bubonic plague that claimed more than 100 lives. During the 1920s, entire streets were demolished in order to make way for the southern approach to the Harbour Bridge, but detailed restoration since 1970 has transformed the district into Sydney's tourist hub, the delights of which are equally appreciated by the locals. The

Clockwise from far left: a view of The Rocks and the bridge from Cahill Expressway; First Impressions *statue at Playfair Street; art works for sale; Aboriginal art displayed at The Rocks Market; street entertainers; historic buildings in The Rocks*

area is packed with attractions, and these will easily fill a day—there are many 1900s buildings to admire, narrow streets such as Nurses Walk and Suez Canal to explore, and plenty of shops and cafés. Campbells Cove, with its historic warehouses next to the Harbour Bridge, and Dawes Point Park under the bridge are both popular waterfront spots. The Rocks also offers many museums and galleries that are well worth visiting.

Sydney Visitor Centre, The Rocks The best place to start is at the Visitor Centre. This information and tour-booking outlet contains a shop and an illuminating display that covers the history of The Rocks. Tours include trips to the Blue Mountains, Hunter Valley and ecotours to the national parks. You can also reserve accommodations and activities, and find out what's on.

THE BASICS

www.therocks.com
D5
Sydney Visitor Centre, The Rocks, corner of Argyle and Playfair streets
8273 0000 or 1800 067 676
Daily 9.30–5.30. Closed Good Friday, 25 Dec
Many cafés and restaurants nearby
Circular Quay
431, 432, 433
Circular Quay
Generally good
Free

More to See

CIRCULAR QUAY

www.sydney.com.au/quay.htm

The focal point of Sydney's maritime life since European settlement, Circular Quay is today a bustling pedestrian precinct with ferry, bus and rail terminals, as well as busy cafés—the perfect spot for a coffee. Be sure to check out the galleries, library and restaurants in nearby Customs House. The covered walkway from the Opera House includes Writers Walk, with plaques commemorating some prominent Australian authors, poets and playwrights. The surrounding precinct of Circular Quay West contains Cadman's Cottage, the city's oldest building (1816). It is now a national parks and wildlife information area (9253 0888). Also in this area is First Fleet Park, commemorating the nation's first settlers, and the large Overseas Passenger Terminal, which received a A$22 million upgrade in 2014.

D5 Circular Quay Cafés and restaurants Circular Quay Various Moderate

CUSTOMS HOUSE

www.sydneycustomshouse.com.au

From 1845 to 1990 this was home to the Customs Service, but today the building's interior is a major cultural venue. There are galleries, a public library and reading room, cafés, studios and a performance space. The lounge area near the grand entrance has WiFi, a TV wall and many magazines.

D5 31 Alfred Street 9242 8551 Mon–Fri 8am–midnight, Sat 10am–midnight, Sun 11–5 Cafés Circular Quay Free

JUSTICE AND POLICE MUSEUM

www.sydneylivingmuseums.com.au

Originally the Water Police Court (1856), these atmospheric old buildings now house a museum of legal and police history. The complex includes the Magistrate's Court, exhibitions in the cells and a museum of crime, the latter featuring mug shots of some of early Sydney's criminals.

D5 Corner Albert and Phillip streets 9252 1144 Sat–Sun 10–5. Closed Good Fri, 25 Dec Nearby Circular Quay Moderate

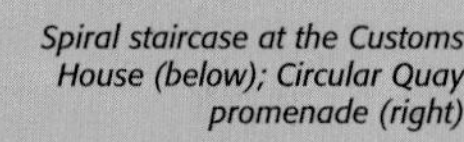

Relaxing at Circular Quay

Spiral staircase at the Customs House (below); Circular Quay promenade (right)

Circular Quay to the Art Gallery

Around the Harbour's edge to see the Opera House, on to the Art Gallery of NSW, via a walk through the Royal Botanic Gardens.

DISTANCE: 4km (2.5 miles) **ALLOW:** 2 hours (plus visits to Opera House and Gallery)

START

CIRCULAR QUAY
D5 Circular Quay

❶ Start your walk from the ferry terminals at Circular Quay and follow the water's edge to the Opera House (▷ 30–31) for great views back toward the Harbour Bridge (▷ 27).

❷ At the Opera House, climb the steps in front and take a guided tour. Walk to Bennelong Point at ground level to watch the passing water-traffic.

❸ Enter the Royal Botanic Gardens (▷ 24–25) at the gate adjacent to the Opera House, and walk along the water around Farm Cove for a way.

❹ Then detour along the garden pathways to see the various plant displays and specimens. Don't miss the tropical plant pyramids at the Macquarie Street end.

❺ Also here is the visitor area (next to Mrs Macquaries Road).

❻ After a look in the visitor area at the botanical exhibitions, pack a picnic to eat in the Gardens before returning to the water's edge and exit the Gardens to check the views from the point at Mrs Macquaries Chair.

❼ Allow plenty of time at the Art Gallery of New South Wales (▷ 72), to view the Australian, Asian and European works of art. The restaurant here, with its views of Woolloomooloo, makes a perfect drink or meal stop. The gallery has an excellent bookshop.

❽ The excellent Yiribana Gallery of Aboriginal and Torres Strait Islander Art displays more than 300 items and changing exhibitions.

END

ART GALLERY OF NEW SOUTH WALES
E6 Sydney Explorer

Shopping

ABORIGINAL ART GALLERIES

www.aboriginalartgalleries.com.au
Displays authentic artworks, craft, ceramics, glass and didgeridoos by various artists.
D5 Shop 13, East Circular Quay, Opera Quays 9251 0511 Circular Quay

ARGYLE GALLERY

www.argylegallery.com.au
Fine Australian and Aboriginal arts and crafts sourced directly from the artists. Paintings, hand-blown glass, bronze animal sculptures, turned wood bowls and boxes, plus some unusual gift ideas, are displayed in a Victorian row house.
D5 21 Playfair Street, The Rocks 9247 4427 Circular Quay

THE AUSTRALIAN WINE CENTRE

www.auswine.com.au
Choose from more than 1,000 Australian wines, including a good range of vintages. They will happily deliver to your hotel, or arrange overseas delivery.
D5 Goldfields House, 3/1 Alfred Street 9247 2755 Circular Quay

BETWEEN THE FLAGS

www.betweentheflags.com.au
Australian beachwear and lifestyle clothing for men, women and children. Shop for trendy tees, hoodies, shorts, trackies, bags and caps.
D5 Shops 1 & 2, Rocks Centre, Argyle Street, The Rocks 9247 2755 Circular Quay

COCOLARTS

www.chocolarts.com.au
Handcrafted chocolates and beautiful edible gifts, made on site using top quality ingredients, including Belgian chocolate and natural Australian flavours.
D5 75 George Street, The Rocks 9817 4222 Circular Quay

CRAFT NSW

www.artsandcraftsnsw.com.au
The Society of Arts and Crafts of NSW sells a range of work by its members at this gallery in the old Coroner's Court. You'll find contemporary Australian craft at its imaginative best.
D5 104 George Street, The Rocks 9241 5825 Circular Quay

SHOPPING TOURS

If you want to shop in the right areas with the aid of local knowledge, or find the best bargains, consider joining a shopping tour. Chic in the City (0416 644337, www.chicinthecity-tours.com.au) offers walking and chauffeur-driven tours to reveal where Sydney's fashionistas shop. Accompanied by a personal stylist, you get the inside track on Australian designers and independent stores.

KEN DUNCAN GALLERY

www.kenduncan.com
Ken Duncan, one of Australia's finest landscape photographers, captures Australia's natural scenery in stunning wide-format images. Framed original works are on display, as well as books of photographs.
D5 73 George Street, The Rocks 9241 3460 Circular Quay

OPAL FIELDS

www.opalfields.com.au
Sydney's largest opal specialist displays fine stones and handcrafted opal jewelry in many beautiful, traditional and contemporary designs.
D5 119 George Street, The Rocks 9247 6800 Circular Quay

OPAL MINDED

www.opalminded.com
The family-owned Jundah mines in Queensland are the source of the black, boulder, light and crystal pipe opals in this shop, where you can buy individual stones or rings, pendants, earrings and cufflinks in distinctive gold or silver settings.
D5 55 George Street, The Rocks 9247 9885 Circular Quay

THE ROCKS

www.therocks.com
The area that's a highlight of any visit to this great city has many fun souvenir shops. In The

Rocks Centre and on George Street, you can buy original artwork and souvenirs, as well as opals, gems, beautiful jewelry and other Australian crafts.
D5 The Rocks Heritage and Visitor Centre 9255 1788 Circular Quay

THE ROCKS CENTRE

A well-designed complex specializing in Australiana, Aboriginal items, arts and crafts and souvenirs.
D5 Argyle Street 9240 8500 Circular Quay

AUSTRALIANA

If you are looking for souvenirs to take home, go for high-quality Australiana. You will find everything from jazzy beachwear to sheepskin products, books on every aspect of Australia, Aboriginal crafts and superb gemstones and jewelry.

THE ROCKS MARKET

More than 150 stalls sell gifts, homeware, antiques and jewelry; there are plenty of cafés, and free entertainment.
D5 George Street, The Rocks 9240 8717 Fri 10–4, Sat–Sun 10–5 Circular Quay

Entertainment and Nightlife

THE BASEMENT

www.thebasement.com.au
This long-established club is the city's best venue for live blues, jazz and swing. The atmosphere is great and there's a Mexican restaurant.
D5 29 Reiby Place 9251 2797 Daily Circular Quay

BLU BAR ON 36

This pricey 36th-floor cocktail bar in one of the city's top hotels provides elegance with astounding views.
D5 Shangri-la Hotel, 176 Cumberland Street, The Rocks 9250 6000 Daily Circular Quay

LORD NELSON BREWERY HOTEL

www.lordnelsonbrewery.com
A visit to Sydney's oldest pub is an absolute must—drinks have been served in this sandstone building since 1841.
C5 19 Kent Street, The Rocks 9251 4044 Daily 431, 432, 433

MODERN AUSTRALIAN

Not so long ago, Australian cooking revolved around meat and three soggy vegetables, plus "sophisticated" dishes like shrimp cocktail and stroganoff. An exciting new Australian modern cuisine has emerged, however, influenced by the eating habits of migrant Italians, Thais, Chinese and others. This experimental cooking might blend French and Thai, or local fish with Lebanese ingredients, to create a great dining experience. Bush tucker—such as kangaroo, crocodile and native plants—is another interesting addition to the Sydney restaurant scene.

MERCANTILE HOTEL

www.themercantilehotel.com.au
This high-spirited renowned Irish pub, established in 1915, is in the cheerful Rocks hotel, famous for its art deco wall tiles, Irish music and draught Guinness.
D4 25 George Street, The Rocks 9247 3570 Daily Circular Quay

TANK STREAM BAR

See and be seen at this bar prefered by workers from the city keen on forgetting the day's hard grind.
D5 1 Tank Stream Way 9240 3100 Mon–Thu 4–late, Fri noon–late, Sat 5–late Circular Quay

Restaurants

PRICES

Prices are approximate, based on a 3-course meal for one person.
$$$ over A$60
$$ A$40–A$60
$ under A$40

BAROQUE ($$)

www.baroquebistro.com.au

Brilliantly French, from the decadence of The Pantry to the modern menu in the Bistro restaurant, it's reasonably priced for the location.

D5 88 George Street, The Rocks 9241 4811 Pantry, Wed–Thu 11.30–3, Fri–Sun 8am-3pm. Bistro Wed–Sat dinner Circular Quay

CAFE SYDNEY ($$$)

www.cafesydney.com

Great location overlooking Circular Quay, a lively cocktail bar serving innovative Australian food and memorable desserts.

D5 Level 5, Customs House, Alfred Street 9251 8683 Mon–Fri and Sun lunch, Mon–Sat dinner Circular Quay

CRUISE BAR ($$)

www.cruisebar.com.au

Signature cocktails, alfresco setting, a fresh, tasty Modern Australian menu and live entertainment in a classy yet casual venue.

D5 Level 1, Overseas Passenger Terminal, West Circular Quay 9251 1188 Daily 11am–late Circular Quay

EST ($$$)

www.merivale.com.au/est

The grand dining room, immaculate service and innovative Australian cuisine highlighting Asian tastes make this the perfect place to celebrate that special occasion.

D5 Level 1, 252 George Street, The Rocks 9240 3010 Mon–Sat dinner Town Hall

GLOBE BAR & BRASSERIE ($$$)

Leather armchairs, velvet sofas, antique books and wood-paneled walls give the air of a private club. Go for Asian delicacies, Western favorites, tasty tapas and the afternoon tea, Tiffin at the Langham.

C5 Langham Hotel, 89–115 Kent Street 9256 2222 Daily noon–10.30 Circular Quay

SYDNEY'S CAFÉ SCENE

A preferred Sydney occupation is hanging out in a café. The drinks, snacks and meals are generally good value, but many establishments offer far more. Outdoor seating, or a view over Bronte Beach, the Opera Hous, or the Harbour are some of the bonuses, while other cafés are in lively areas like The Rocks, Bondi, or inner-city Darlinghurst. Sydney's coffee, thanks to European influences, is usually excellent.

HICKSONS FOOD & WINE ($$)

www.hicksons.com

Informal indoor/outdoor wine bar patronized by the Wharf Theatre crowd. Specializes in seasonal dishes to share. The Walsh Bay area has a great atmosphere.

C5 Pier 7, 17 Hickson Road, Walsh Bay 9241 2031 Tue–Sat, lunch and dinner 431

LOWENBRAU KELLER($$)

www.lowenbrau.com.au

You'll find traditional Bavarian fare here including chicken schnitzel, pork knuckle and cheese spätzle, as well as delicious pastries and a variety of beers.

D5 18 Argyle Street, The Rocks 9247 7785 Daily, breakfast, lunch and dinner Circular Quay

MCA CAFÉ ($$)

www.mca.com.au

Modern Australian menu with delicious seafood dishes, soups, salads, sandwiches, a kids' menu plus a comprehensive wine list and great views of the Harbour. Highlight tables are on the Sculpture terrace.

D5 MCA, 140 George Street, The Rocks 9250 8443 Daily 10–4 (Thu to 9pm) Circular Quay

MOS CAFÉ ($$)

Very popular with city workers for breakfast.

Lunch and dinner feature great modern creations such as salt-and-pepper squid and chargrilled Junee lamb.
D5 37 Phillip Street 9241 3636 Mon–Fri breakfast, lunch and dinner, Sat–Sun breakfast, lunch Circular Quay

MR WONG ($$)
www.merivale.com.au/mrwong
You can be sure to get authentic Cantonese dishes and the best dim sum in this big and popular restaurant with colonial-style decor.
D5 3 Bridge Lane 9240 3000 Daily lunch and dinner Wynyard

NEPTUNE PALACE ($$–$$$)
www.neptunepalace.com
Come here for good Chinese/Malaysian cuisine with dishes such as *lakas*, Malay curries, Penang-style chicken and tasty seafood dishes.
D5 Level 1, Gateway Building, corner Pitt and Alfred streets, Circular Quay 9241 3338 Daily lunch, dinner Circular Quay

Q DINING ($$$)
www.pullmanquaygrandsydneyharbour.com
Enjoy great Circular Quay views while you dine in this light and airy contemporary setting. Local and indigenous spices enhance local cuisine.
E5 Pullman Quay Grand Sydney Harbour 9256 4040 Daily breakfast, Mon–Fri lunch, Sat dinner, Sat–Sun high tea Circular Quay

QUAY ($$$)
www.quay.com.au
On the S. Pellegrino World's 50 Best Restaurants list, seafood is a specialty at the award-winning Quay. Fantastic Harbour views.
D5 Upper level, Overseas Passenger Terminal, Circular Quay West 9251 5600 Mon–Fri lunch, daily dinner Circular Quay

QUAY BAR ($)
www.quaybar.com.au
Excellent food, boutique tap beers, imaginative cocktails and an international range of wines with house salads, burgers and pies for bistro fare.
D5 Ground floor, Customs House, Alfred Street, Circular Quay 9247 4898 Mon–Fri 7.30am–late, Sat 9am–1am Circular Quay

IDEAL SETTING

For top-quality dining in the most spectacular of settings at the Harbour edge, try Aria ($$$). Chef owner Matt Moran's award-winning menus, exquisitely presented food and extensive wine list combine to create an occasion to savour.
D5 1 Macquarie Street, East Circular Quay 9240 2255 Mon–Fri lunch, dinner daily, also pre-theater and supper menus Circular Quay

ROCKPOOL ($$–$$$)
www.rockpool.com
Rockpool continues its reign as Sydney's best seafood restaurant, chef Neil Perry presenting his signature dishes with flair. Oysters served in the bar.
D5 11 Bridge Street, The Rocks 9252 1888 Mon–Fri lunch, Mon–Sat dinner Wynyard

SAILORS THAI ($$–$$$)
This Rocks eaterie serves famously good food. Go to the Canteen for an informal lunch or dinner at the communal table by the busy open kitchen, or reserve a table in the elegant dining room for excellent Thai classics and fine wines.
D5 106 George Street, The Rocks 9251 2466 Canteen: Mon–Fri lunch, dinner daily. Dining Room: Fri lunch, Tue–Sat dinner Circular Quay

SIR STAMFORD AT CIRCULAR QUAY ($$)
www.stamford.com.au
The fabulously indulgent Sydney High Tea is served among the antiques of this elegant boutique hotel. The tea is a delicious mix of savory and sweet offerings, with a tea menu to dream about and ponder over. Reservations for High Tea are essential.
D5 93 Macquarie Street 9252 4600 High tea served daily from 11am, last booking 4pm Circular Quay

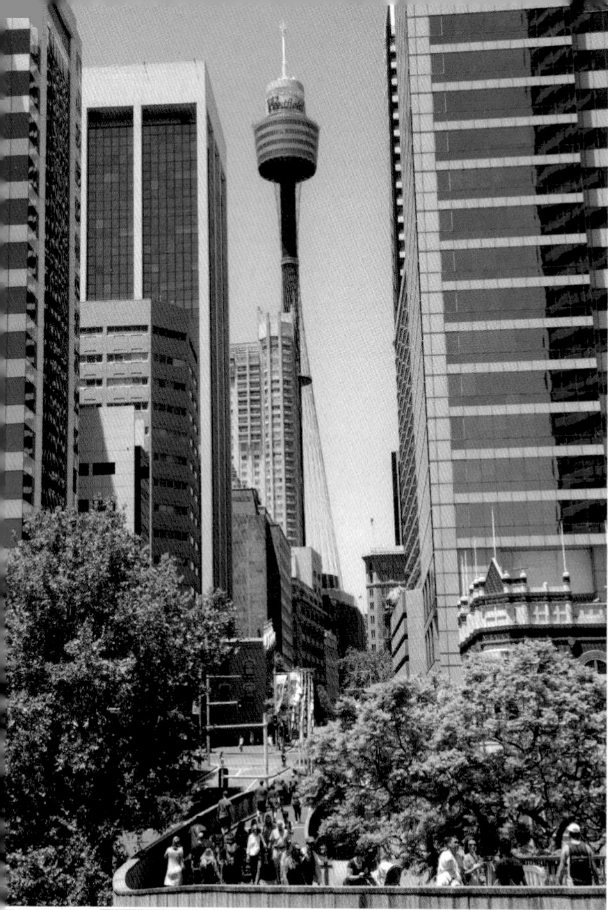

Darling Harbour and Pyrmont

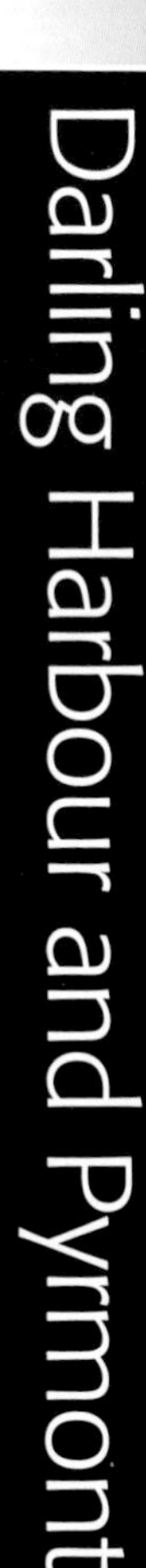

As the recreational hub of the city, Darling Harbour and Pyrmont are very busy on the weekends, when families come to enjoy the exhibitions, attractions and entertainment on offer.

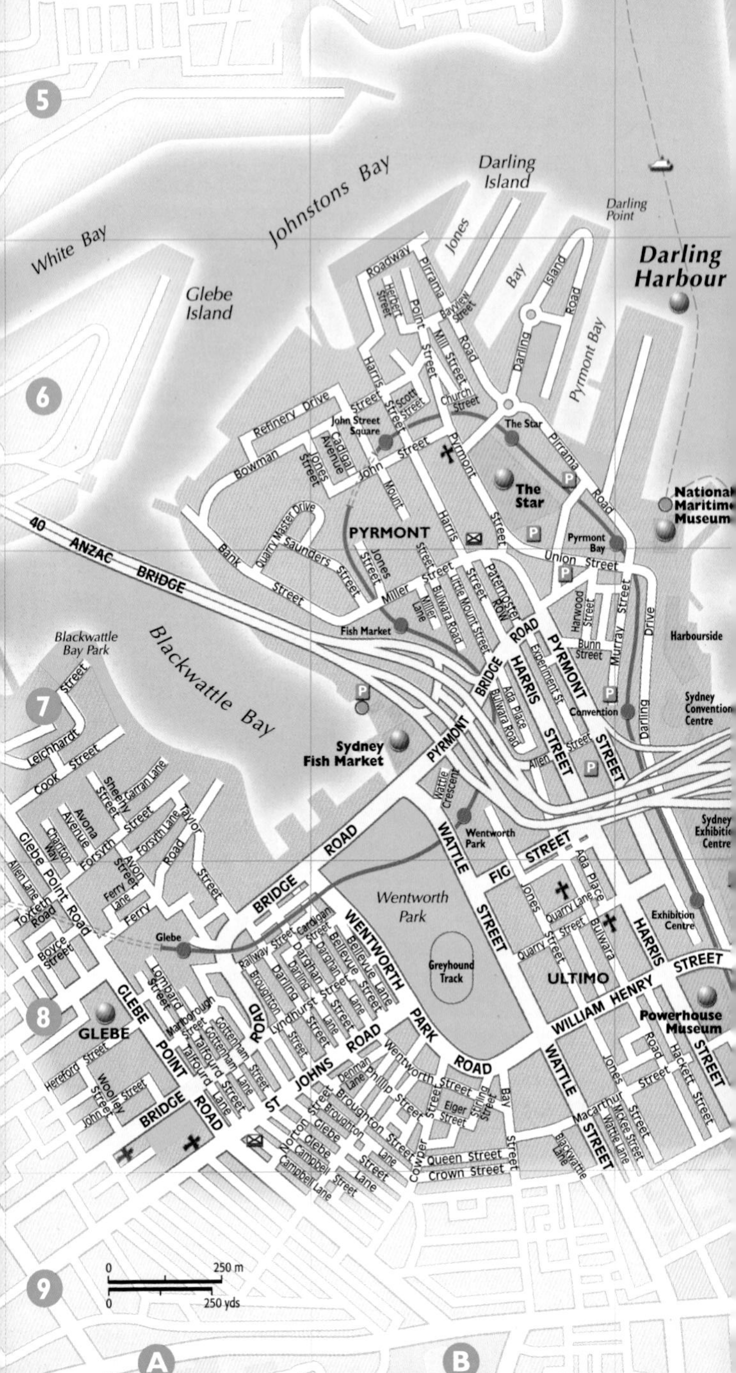

Johnstons Bay
White Bay
Glebe Island
Darling Island
Darling Point
Darling Harbour
Jones Bay
Pyrmont Bay
National Maritime Museum
The Star
PYRMONT
ANZAC BRIDGE
Blackwattle Bay Park
Blackwattle Bay
Sydney Fish Market
Fish Market
John Street Square
Pyrmont Bay
Convention
Harbourside
Sydney Convention Centre
Sydney Exhibition Centre
Exhibition Centre
Wentworth Park
Greyhound Track
ULTIMO
Powerhouse Museum
Glebe
GLEBE
0
250 m
0
250 yds
5
6
7
8
9
A
B

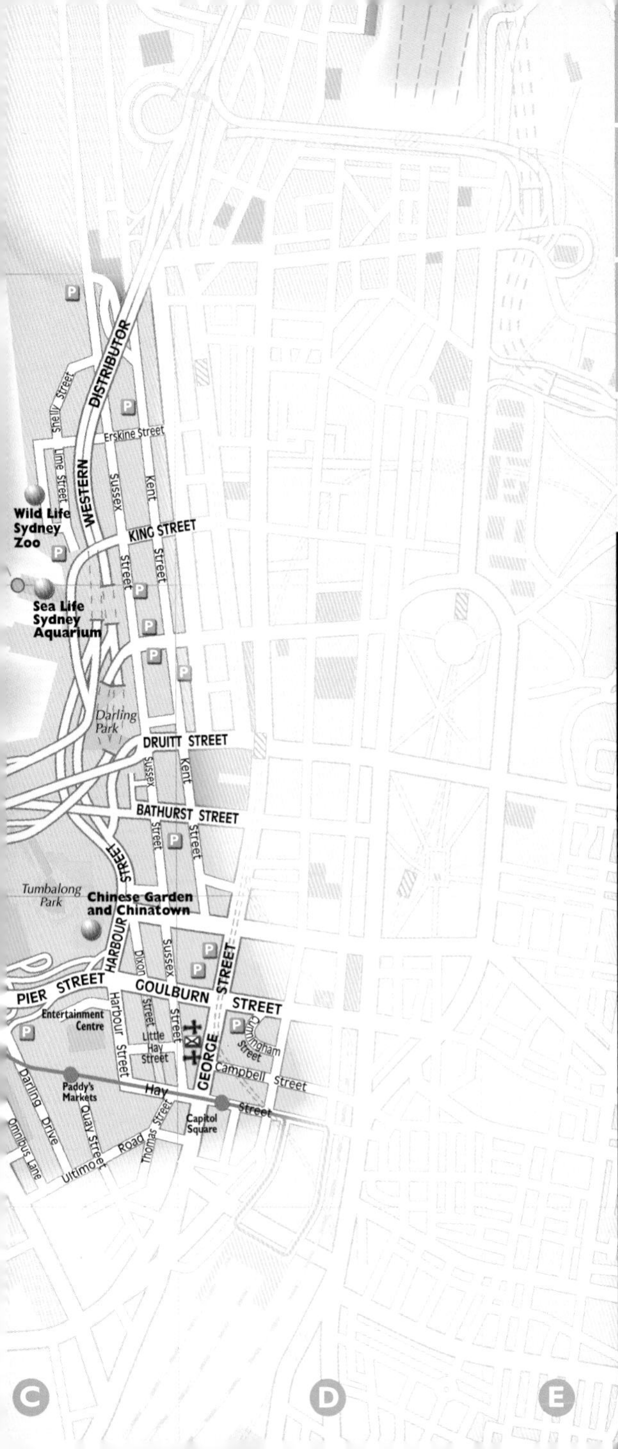

Darling Harbour and Pyrmont

Chinese Garden and Chinatown

TOP 25

HIGHLIGHTS

- Garden's pavilions, lakes and waterfalls
- Quantas Credit Union Arena
- Paddy's Markets (▷ 63)
- Dixon Street
- Capitol Theatre (▷ 64)

TIP

- Check out the many specialty shops for Asian cooking ingredients and herbal remedies.

The vibrant Chinese quarter, part of the city since the 1860s, is a great place for Asian cuisines and specialty shopping. The Chinese Garden, just a few steps from Chinatown, offers a calm retreat in the middle of busy downtown Sydney.

The Chinese Garden The largest of its kind outside mainland China, this tranquil garden was designed by Chinese landscape architects from Guangdong Province, a New South Wales sister state, and features Cantonese-style pavilions, lakes, waterfalls and bridges. With its shrubs, flowers and trees, including maples, this is a delightful spot in which to relax after seeing Darling Harbour's myriad attractions. Its other name is the Garden of Friendship, symbolizing the enduring links between China and Australia. The

Clockwise from far left: Cantonese-style pavilions in the Chinese Garden; Chinese dragon statue; ponds and lakes are a feature of the gardens; detail of a carved wall plaque; carp pond; Chinese New Year procession in Sydney's Chinatown

garden offers a calm retreat from the hustle and bustle of the city. A teahouse serves traditional Chinese tea, dim sum and other refreshments.

Chinatown On Dixon, Hay and Sussex streets, Sydney's Chinatown is a bustling area of Asian food and clothing shops, as well as moderately priced restaurants. Paddy's Markets are held here from Thursday to Sunday and the area includes the city's largest performance venue, the Quantas Credit Union Arena (▷ 64). The beautifully restored 1928 Capitol Theatre, home of major musical and theatrical events, is nearby on Campbell Street; it's worth seeing a show to appreciate the fine ornate interior. Chinese New Year (January or February) is a particularly exciting time to be in the area, when you will see fireworks, dragon dances and street processions.

THE BASICS

www.chinesegarden.com.au
C8
Chinese Garden, Pier Street, Darling Harbour
Chinese Garden 9240 8888
Daily 9.30–dusk. CLosed Good Fri, 25 Dec
Cafés and restaurants nearby
Town Hall
333, 433, 555
Light rail to Paddy's Market Station
King's Wharf, Darling Harbour
Good
Inexpensive

National Maritime Museum

TOP 25

The museum's water-side location (left); interior exhibition space (below)

THE BASICS

www.anmm.gov.au
C6
2 Murray Street, Darling Harbour
9298 3777
Daily 9.30–5 (to 6pm in Jan); closed 25 Dec
Good café, picnic tables
Town Hall
443
Light Rail to Pyrmont Bay
Pyrmont Bay Wharf
Excellent
Galleries: expensive; Big Ticket: expensive
The Store book and gift shop

HIGHLIGHTS

- HMAS *Vampire*
- Hands-on exhibits
- Vietnamese refugee boat
- HMB *Endeavour*
- US Gallery
- Navy submarine
- *Spirit of Australia*

This comprehensive display of Australia's maritime heritage, from the arrival of the First Fleet to the modern voyages of Vietnamese boat people, documents Australia's various links with the ocean.

Indoor displays The museum features eight themed sections—Eora: First People, Navigators, On the waterfront, Commerce, Passengers, Sport and Play, Navy and Linked by the Sea—that contain thousands of items in displays as diverse as early beach fashions, the globe-circling yacht *Blackmore's First Lady* and migrant voyages. Other highlights include a section on Aboriginal people and the sea, the maritime links between Australia and the US and an intriguing display on how a Sydney man built the world's fastest boat, *Spirit of Australia,* in his back garden. Temporary exhibitions are also presented regularly.

Outdoor displays Once you've seen what's on offer inside, go to the outdoor displays, moored at the museum's wharves. The historic vessels include HMAS *Vampire*, the last of the Royal Australian Navy's big gunships, and HMAS *Onslow* one of the navy's submarines, both of which you can tour. Among the other interesting craft here are the *Akarana*, an 1888 racing cutter, a Vietnamese refugee boat that reached northern Australia, a lugger from the pearling port of Broome in Western Australia and *Krait*, used in a commando operation in WWII. A replica of the HMB *Endeavour*, Captain Cook's famous vessel, is often moored at the wharf for visitors to explore.

Spacewalking in the Powerhouse Museum (left); restored steam train (right)

TOP 25 Powerhouse Museum

Sydney's most innovative museum is housed in a cavernous old power station with modern extensions. Interactive audiovisual displays are combined with fascinating historical exhibits.

The building During the 1980s the 1899 Ultimo Power Station was transformed into Sydney's largest museum. Displays are housed in the vast boiler, turbine and engine houses, as well as the Neville Wran Building, which was inspired by grand 19th-century halls and rail stations.

The collection The award-winning museum contains much of the Museum of Applied Arts and Sciences' extensive collection, which originated in the 1880s. The contents range from the enormous 18th-century Boulton and Watt steam engine to historic gowns, from transport to ecology for a sustainable future, nuclear matters, cyberworlds, shopping in Australia 1880–1930, experiments in scientific principles and computers. There are also audiovisual presentations, sound effects, holograms and dozens of hands-on scientific displays. You can even sit in King's Cinema, a re-creation of a 1930s art deco cinema and watch a silent movie, accompanied by the bells, whistles and gadgetry of an electrically and air-activated Fotoplayer. Visit the shop for its range of books, gifts and interesting souvenirs.

Children welcome The museum is a wonderland for youngsters, with many activities and hands-on explorations geared especially for them.

THE BASICS

www.powerhousemuseum.com
C8
500 Harris Street, Ultimo
9217 0111
Daily 10–5; closed 25 Dec
Courtyard café
Central
422, M30
Light Rail to Paddy's Markets
Aquarium Wharf, Darling Harbour
Excellent
Moderate

HIGHLIGHTS

- Decorative Arts section
- Boulton and Watt engine
- King's Cinema
- "Space: Beyond this World"
- Transportation section
- Cyberworlds
- Free WiFi

Sea Life Sydney Aquarium and Darling Harbour

HIGHLIGHTS

- Sharks in "The Open Ocean"
- Great Barrier Reef display
- Saltwater crocodiles
- Touch pool
- Marine Mammal Sanctuary
- Pyrmont Bridge

TIP

- The Aquarium can be crowded on weekends and during school holidays.

Encounter sharks and crocodiles at close quarters, marvel at the species diversity of the Great Barrier Reef and explore Australia's marine environments at this world-class aquarium.

Aquatic fun The real thrill here is walking through transparent plastic tunnels beneath the two vast floating oceanariums, watching schools of magnificent tropical fish, rays, eels and sharks glide above you. The Great Barrier Reef display features fish and coral that are vivid colours, while the saltwater crocodiles are awesome. Seals frolic in the Marine Mammal Sanctuary and children can handle marine creatures in the touch pool.

Darling Harbour The eastern part of Darling Harbour offers several attractions, including the

Children watching sharks in Sea Life Sydney Aquarium (left); the twinkling lights of Darling Harbour at dusk (below)

IMAX Theatre, with the world's biggest screen, housed in a distinctive eye-shaped building.

Cockle Bay Wharf On the city side of Darling Harbour is a food and entertainment precinct, open daily until late. To the north of Cockle Bay there's Wild Life Sydney Zoo (▷ 62), sited next to the Aquarium. Here you'll see more than 6,000 Australian animals living in their natural habitats and some of Australia's deadliest snakes. Have lunch at King Street Wharf, a few minutes' walk farther north. Nearby Pyrmont Bridge (1902), which links the two sides of Darling Harbour, is the world's oldest electrically operated swingspan bridge and is still in use. Across the bridge is the National Maritime Museum (▷ 58) on your right, and Harbourside (▷ 63), a huge dining and a shopping complex, on your left.

THE BASICS

www.sydneyaquarium.com.au

C6, C7

Sydney Aquarium and Wild Life Sydney Zoo, Aquarium Pier. IMAX Theatre, Aquarium Wharf, Darling Harbour

Aquarium 1 800 199657 (daily 9–5); Wild Life Sydney Zoo 9333 9288; IMAX Theatre 9281 3300

Aquarium daily 9.30–7; IMAX Theatre daily 10–10

Aquarium cafés

Town Hall

Any bus to Market or King Street

Light rail to Convention Centre

Aquarium Wharf

Very good

Expensive

More to See

GLEBE

Glebe offers offbeat shopping, a Saturday market and the superb Nicholson Museum with its famous archaeological collection at the University of Sydney.

A8 Museum 9351 2812 Museum Mon–Fri 10–4.30; closed public holidays Cafés and restaurants 413 Free

THE STAR

www.star.com.au

A vast and glittering entertainment venue with views of the Harbour and city, The Star boasts over 20 restaurants, bars and cafés, a boutique hotel, day spa, nightclub, upscale shops and a luxuriously appointed casino floor. Here, gamblers can try their luck at blackjack, roulette, poker, *pai gow*, *mah jong*, baccarat and 1,500 slot machines. The 2,000-seat Lyric Theatre (▷ 64) is also here, plus a sparkling rooftop Event Centre that hosts international stars and A-list acts in concert settings.

B6 80 Pyrmont Street, Pyrmont 9777 9000 Daily 24 hours Numerous restaurants and cafés Town Hall, Light Rail to The Star 43 Pyrmont Bay Wharf Free entry

SYDNEY FISH MARKET

Come to admire (and buy if you are going to a barbecue!) the vast range of fresh seafood and to sample the great fish and French fries. Also fruit, vegetables and deli items.

B7 Bank Street, Pyrmont 9660 1611 Daily 7–4 Light Rail to Fish Market 443, 501

WILD LIFE SYDNEY ZOO

www.wildlifesydney.com.au

Some 6,000 Australian animals, including wallabies, possums, quolls, koalas, possums and many deadly snakes, housed in nine replicated habitats. Check the website for daily feeding times and informative talks.

C6 Aquarium Pier, Darling Harbour 1800 206 158 Daily Apr–Oct 9.30–5; Nov–Mar 9.30–8 All buses to King Street Light Rail to Convention or Pyrmont Bay Aquarium Pier Expensive

Browsing at Gleebooks store in Glebe

Catch of the day at the Sydney Fish Market

Shopping

BALMAIN MARKET

www.balmainmarket.com.au

With shoppers ranging from punks to aging hippies, this market (held on the grounds of an old church) has a pleasant community feel. Browse for arts and crafts and, in the church hall, try the vegetarian food.

B4 Corner of Darling Street and Curtis Road, Balmain 9818 1791 Sat 8.30–4 442, 445 Darling Street

CHINATOWN AND HAYMARKET

This area is home to many Asian food shops, dozens of cafés and restaurants and inexpensive clothes stores. Lively and cosmopolitan.

C8 South of Goulburn Street Central

CROCODILE SHOP

www.darlingharbour.com/shop/crocodile-shop.aspx

Possum, alpaca and merino wool feature with sheepskin, crocodile and kangaroo skin products that range from bags to belts to hats and wraps.

C7 Level 1, shop 113, Harbourside, Darling Harbour 9211 7920 Light Rail to Pyrmont Bay Central

GLEBE MARKETS

www.glebemarkets.com.au

Around 200 outdoor stalls with clothing and fashion items, crafts and collectibles. Many interesting shops and some great cafés are nearby.

B9 Glebe Public School, Glebe Point Road, Glebe 0419 291 449 Sat 10–4 431, 433

GLEEBOOKS

www.gleebooks.com.au

An excellent bookshop in the inner-west suburb of Glebe, close to the University of Sydney. Great for browsing. Gleebooks (Kids), also in Glebe Road, specialises in children's books.

B9 49 Glebe Point Road, Glebe 9660 2333 431

HARBOURSIDE DARLING HARBOUR

www.harbourside.com.au

Darling Harbour's shopping complex is vast—more than 150 shops, selling fashion items, souvenirs, CDs and tapes, jewelry and many other goods.

C7 Darling Harbour 8204 1888 Light Rail to Pyrmont Bay

BARGAIN SHOPPING

The best shopping bargains are found at sales times—after Christmas and into January and again at the end of winter in July and August. You can shop for budget clothing at any time in Surry Hills, Sydney's rag trade area, and at Redfern, where designer outfits and other clothes are very reasonably priced. Inner-west Newtown (especially King Street) offers bargains in secondhand clothing and many other items. In the city, be sure to check out Market City near Chinatown for bargains galore from the hundreds of stall operators who regularly trade here.

PADDY'S MARKETS

www.paddysmarkets.com.au

Sydney's biggest and oldest market, with more than 1,000 stalls under cover, selling everything from clothes and books to jewelry and vegetables. Great for bargain hunters.

C8 Corner of Thomas and Hay streets, Haymarket 9325 6200 Wed–Sun 9–5 Light Rail to Paddy's Markets

SUSSEX CENTRE

Excellent food court for a wide range of inexpensive Asian meals, plus Chinese herbalists, reflexology areas, Asian antiques and crafts and shops with exotic cooking ingredients and homewares.

C8 401 Sussex Street, Haymarket 9281 6388 443 Light Rail to Capitol Square

THAI-KEE SUPERMARKET

An Asian supermarket in Chinatown, featuring a butcher's section, exotic fruit and vegetables, and spices and ingredients for Chinese, Malaysian, Thai and Vietnamese cooking.

C8 393 Sussex Street 9281 2202 Central

Entertainment and Nightlife

CAPITOL THEATRE

www.capitoltheatre.com.au

Refurbishment has made the 2,000-seat Capitol, dating from 1928, Sydney's most glorious performance space. Home of musicals and major theatrical events.

D8 13 Campbell Street, Haymarket 1300 558 878 Central (Railway Square exit)

CARGO BAR AND LOUNGE

www.cargobar.com.au thecargolounge.com.au

Enjoy a sunset beer or cocktail in the outdoor beer garden or the split-level, waterside bar. On Friday you can dance from dusk until dawn.

C7 52–60 The Promenade, King Street Wharf 8070 2424 Daily 11am–late Town Hall 412, 413 Aquarium Pier

CHERRY

www.star.com.au

A cocktail bar with city views and dance sounds that span house, disco, Balearic beat and lounge DJ mixes.

B6 Level 1, Casino, The Star, 80 Pyrmont Street 1800 700 700 Wed–Thu 5pm–12, Fri 4pm–1am, Sat 4pm–2am Light Rail to The Star Pyrmont Bay Wharf

HARBOUR JET

www.harbourjet.com

Extreme Harbour tours by jet boat. A choice of the 35-minute Jet Blast Adventure (includes spins and power brake stops) or the slightly more sedate 50-minute Sydney Harbour Adventure. Photo opportunities and music.

C7 50B The Promenade, King Street Wharf 1300 887 373 Daily Convention

HOME

www.homesydney.com

Several bars, views of Darling Harbour and, best of all, three levels of dance featuring funk, house, techno and garage.

C7 101/1 Wheat Road, Cockle Bay Wharf, Darling Harbour 9266 0600 Fri–Sun; see website for events Town Hall

WATERING HOLES

Drinking is a very popular pastime in Sydney and there are countless bars and pubs to visit. In addition to the well-known Foster's and VB beers, there are more unusual brands such as Redback, Hahn and Coopers. Australia's local spirit is Bundaberg rum "Bundy", available in underproof and the lethal overproof varieties. Beer is generally served in "middies" (284ml/10fl oz glasses) and larger "schooners". Bars and pubs, some of which are in hotels, are licensed to trade for varying hours each day but are generally open until at least 11pm, while nightclubs and discos stay open longer.

LYRIC THEATRE

www.sydneylyric.com.au

This modern theater presents big musicals and a variety of internationally acclaimed performances.

B6 Pirrama Road, Pyrmont 9509 3600; tickets 1300 795 267 443 Light Rail to The Star

PONTOON

www.pontoonbar.com

This trendy bar and nightclub overlooking Darling Harbour has futuristic decor and a waterside restaurant open for lunch and dinner. Pontoon Fridays sees DJs spinning house, hiphop and RnB from 6pm. Check the website for drinks specials.

C7 The Promenade, Cockle Bay Wharf, Darling Harbour 9267 7099 Daily 11.30am–late Town Hall

QANTAS CREDIT UNION ARENA

www.qantascreditunionarena.com.au

Formerly the Sydney Entertainment Centre, the city's largest venue hosts everything from concerts by touring international rock groups to indoor tennis and basketball matches.

C8 Harbour Street, Haymarket 9320 4200 Performances most days Light Rail to Haymarket

Restaurants

PRICES

Prices are approximate, based on a 3-course meal for one person.

$$$ over A$60
$$ A$40–A$60
$ under A$40

CAFFE OTTO ($–$$)

www.cafeottoglebe.com

This bright and cheerful café serves good soups, pasta and snacks and totally decadent cakes and desserts. BYO.

B9 79 Glebe Point Road, Glebe 9552 1519 Daily snacks, lunch and dinner 431

CHINATOWN CENTRE ($)

One of Sydney's many self-service food halls—choose from all types of Asian food. Licensed.

C8 25 Dixon Street, Haymarket 9212 3335 Daily 10–10 Town Hall

FISHERMAN'S WHARF ($)

www.fishermanswharf.com.au

You can handpick your seafood from the tanks of this Chinese restaurant. It has plenty to please meat-eaters, too.

B7 Level 1, Bank Street, Pyrmont 9660 9888 Daily lunch, dinner 443, 501l

GOLDEN CENTURY ($$)

www.goldencentury.com.au

This busy Chinese eatery, in the heart of Chinatown, specializes in the freshest seafood.

C8 393–399 Sussex Street, Haymarket 9231 1598 Daily lunch, dinner Central (take the Railway Square exit)

THE MALAYA ($–$$)

www.themalaya.com.au

One of the longest-established and best Asian restaurants in town, serving a tempting array of Indonesian, Malaysian and Chinese.

C6 39 Lime Street (Kings Street Wharf) 9279 1170 Daily dinner, Mon–Sat lunch Sydney Aquarium

PEPINO'S ($)

www.pepinos.com.au

This excellent licensed Mexican restaurant offers an authentic range of combo plates, *fajitas* and seafood dishes, using high-quality ingredients.

AUSTRALIAN SEAFOOD

It is not surprising that seafood is so popular in this oceanside city. Local specialties include Sydney rock oysters, while kingfish, enormous shrimps, Tasmanian scallops and smoked salmon, South Australian tuna and northern fish such as the delicious barramundi grace menus all over town. Appropriately, many seafood restaurants have waterfront locations and you can also enjoy excellent take-out food.

Off map 181 Victoria Road, Gladesville 9817 1988 Tue–Sun dinner only 501, 518, 520

QUARRYMAN'S HOTEL ($)

www.quarrymanshotel.com.au

Australian craft beers on tap with bar food plus a proper dining space upstairs offering seafood, burgers, steak, pies, pasta and nachos.

B7 216 Harris Street, Pyrmont 8710 3551 Daily lunch, dinner 501

SAPPHO BOOKS CAFE & WINE BAR ($–$$)

www.sapphobooks.com.au

Heaven for lovers of books and good coffee. The courtyard café has vegetarian and vegan options on the menu and morphs into a wine bar in the evening.

B9 51 Glebe Point Road, Glebe 9552 4498 Café Mon–Sat 7.30–6, Sun 9–6.30. Wine bar Wed–Sat 6pm–late 431

SOKYO ($$$)

www.star.com.au/sokyo

Fine dining, modern Japanese style. Bold tastes in beautifully crafted and presented dishes Pre-theater dining and the lunch special on Fridays are good value.

B6 Level g, The Darling, The Star, 80 Pyrmont Street 9657 9161 Mon–Sat dinner (lunch also Fri) Light Rail to The Star Pyrmont Bay Wharf

CBD and East Sydney

The Central Business District is home to many major companies and associated legal and financial services, as well as the city's top hotels. Its retail heart includes charming old arcades, the Queen Victoria Building and the major department stores.

WYNYARD
Erskine Street
CLARENCE
YORK
GEORGE
STREET
O'Connell Street
Bligh Street
Bent Street
Phillip Street
Hunter Street
Chifley Tower
State Library of New South Wales
State Parliament House
Sydney Hospital
The Mint Museum
Martin Place
MARTIN PLACE
MACQUARIE
Pitt
Castlereagh
The Landmark
KING STREET
King Street
Queens Square
Art Gallery of New South Wales
Hyde Park Barracks
CAHILL EXPRESSWAY
Cowper
Bland Street
Nicholson Street
Wilson
Griffiths Street
Best Street
Dowling
Sydney Tower and Skywalk
City Centre
Market Street
St James Road
ST JAMES
PRINCE ALBERT ROAD
St Marys Road
St Mary's Cathedral
Sir John Young Crescent
Queen Victoria Building
Wesley Chapel Theatre
Elizabeth
Hyde Park
Cathedral Street
Sylvia Chase Square
Yurong Parkway
Boomerang Street
Riley Street
Crown
Palmer
Bourke
WOOLLOOMOO
TOWN HALL
DRUITT STREET
Town Hall
PARK STREET
St Andrew's Cathedral
BATHURST STREET
Bathurst Street
Australian Museum
COLLEGE
WILLIAM STREET
Yurong Lane
Crown Lane
Rosella Lane
Judge Street
KINGS CROSS
Wilmot Street
Central Street
Telstra Plaza
MUSEUM
Anzac War Memorial
Stanley Street
Francis Lane
Francis Street
Chapel Street
Premier Lane
Clapton Place
Farrell Avenue
DARLINGHURST
LIVERPOOL
STREET
ELIZABETH
Whitlam Square
Clarke St
Civic Tower
Liverpool Street
Kings Lane
Thomson
Forbes
Liverpool Street
Darlinghurst
Darley
Hardie St
GOULBURN STREET
Alberta St
WENTWORTH AVENUE
Poplar Street
Pelican Street
OXFORD
Foy Lane
Brisbane
Goulburn Street
Burton Street
Hunt Street
Foster Street
Commonwealth
Campbell
Taylor Square
Victoria
Foley
Reservoir Street
Batman Lane
Smith Street
Mackey
Ann Street
Mary
Wright Lane
Denham
Sturt Street
Taylor St
Chisholm Street
BOUNDARY
FLINDERS STREET
SOUTH DOWLING STREET
West Street
Little Albion Street
Albion
Terry St
Mary Street
Commonwealth Street
Albion Way
Belmore Street
Bellevue Street
Waterloo Street
SURRY HILLS
Jesmond Street
Short Street
Hill Street
Napier Street
University of New South Wales
Albion Avenue
Fitzroy Street
FOVEAUX STREET
Sophia Street
Kippax Street
Lacey Street
Nichols Street
Hutchinson Street
Seymour Pl
Selwyn
Iris Street
Greens Road
FITZROY STREET
Griffin St
Norton St
Collins Street
Richards La
Richards Avenue
Bennett Place
Marshall Street
Bennett Street
Josephson Street
Prospect Street
Withers La
Collins Lane
Alexander Street
Phelps Street
Arthur Street
Tudor Street
Rainford Street
Davies Street
Brett Whiteley Studio
Nobbs Street
Olivia Lane
Parkham Street
Mort Street
Moore Park
ANZAC PARADE
CLEVELAND STREET
0
250 m
0
250 yds
6
7
8
9
10
11
C
D
E

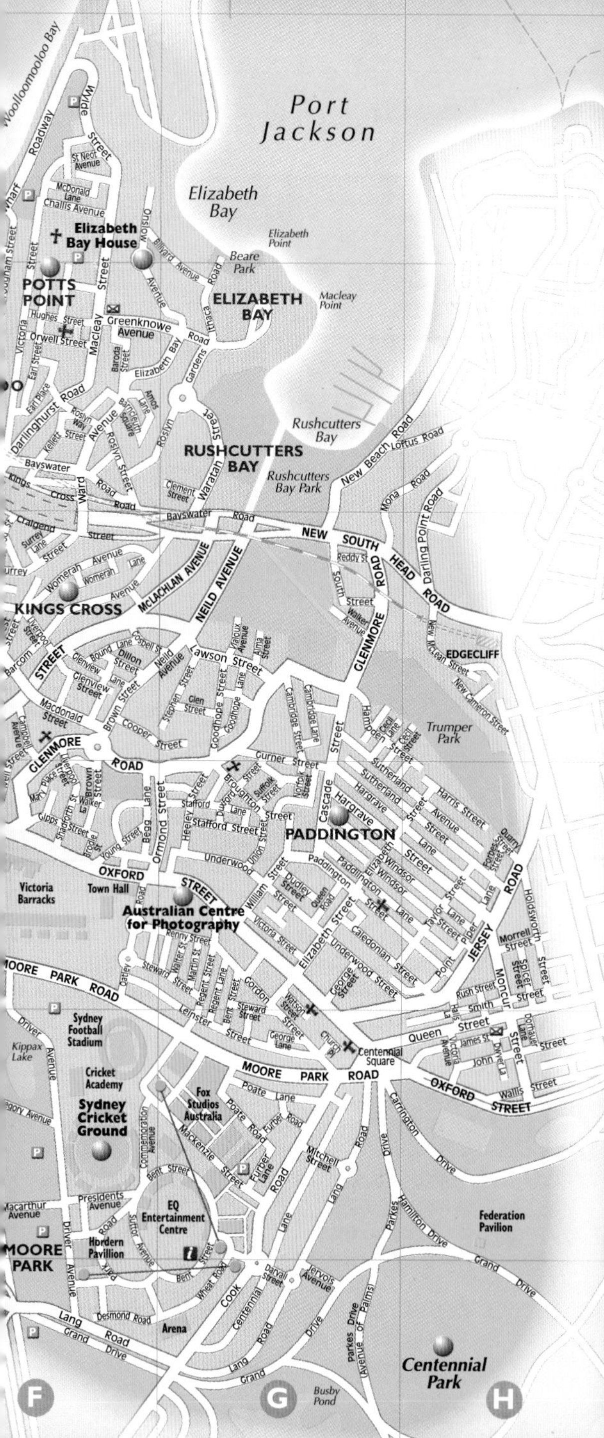

Port Jackson
Woolloomooloo Bay
Elizabeth Bay
Elizabeth Point
Beare Park
Macleay Point
Rushcutters Bay
Rushcutters Bay Park
POTTS POINT
ELIZABETH BAY
RUSHCUTTERS BAY
KINGS CROSS
EDGECLIFF
PADDINGTON
Elizabeth Bay House
Trumper Park
Victoria Barracks
Town Hall
Australian Centre for Photography
Sydney Football Stadium
Kippax Lake
Cricket Academy
Sydney Cricket Ground
Fox Studios Australia
EQ Entertainment Centre
Hordern Pavillion
Arena
MOORE PARK
Centennial Square
Federation Pavilion
Centennial Park
Busby Pond
Wylde Street
Cowper Wharf Roadway
St Neot Avenue
McDonald Lane
Challis Avenue
Onslow Avenue
Billyard Avenue
Ithaca Road
Hughes Street
Orwell Street
Victoria Street
Macleay Street
Greenknowe Avenue
Baroda Street
Elizabeth Bay Road
Gardens
Earl Street
Earl Place
Darlinghurst Road
Roslyn Avenue
Roslyn Way
Roslyn Street
Kellett Street
Baroda Square
Amos Lane
Waratah Street
Clement Street
Bayswater Road
Kings Cross Road
Ward Avenue
Craigend Street
Surrey Lane
Womerah Avenue
Womerah Lane
McLachlan Avenue
Neild Avenue
New South Head Road
New Beach Road
Loftus Road
Mona Road
Darling Point Road
Reddy St
South Street
Walker Avenue
Glenmore Road
New McLean Street
New Cameron Street
Liverpool Street
Barcom Avenue
Bound Lane
Dillon Street
Gosbell St
Glenview Street
Glenview Lane
Brown Street
Macdonald Street
Campbell Avenue
Cooper Street
Lawson Street
Valoux Avenue
Alma Street
Glen Street
Goodhope Street
Stephen Street
Cambridge Street
Cambridge Lane
Hampden Street
Cecil Lane
Cecil Street
Gurner Street
Sutherland Street
Sutherland Avenue
Hargrave Lane
Harris Street
Quarry Street
Forbes Street
Broughton Street
Suffolk Street
Norfolk Street
Cascade Street
Mary Place
Walker La
Gipps Street
Shadforth St
Brodie St
Young Street
Begg Lane
Ormond Street
Heeley Street
Stafford Lane
Stafford Street
Dowling Lane
Union Street
Underwood Street
Paddington Street
Elizabeth Street
Windsor Street
Windsor Lane
Taylor Street
Piper Lane
Jersey Road
Oxford Street
William Street
Dudley Street
Queen Road
Victoria Street
Renny Street
Caledonian Street
Morrell Street
Holdsworth Street
Spicer Street
Moncur Street
Point Road
Oatley Road
Steward Street
Walter St
Martin St
Regent Street
Regent Lane
Bent Street
Gordon Street
George Street
George Lane
Underwood Street
Watson Street
Church Pl
Leinster Street
Rush Street
Smith Street
Hills La
Queen Street
Victoria Avenue
James St
Dwyer La
Donahue Lane
John Street
Wallis Street
Moore Park Road
Driver Avenue
Poate Lane
Poate Road
Furber Road
Furber Lane
Mackenzie Street
Commemoration Avenue
Mitchell Street
Lang Road
Carrington Drive
Parkes Drive
Hamilton Drive
Grand Drive
Presidents Avenue
Gregory Avenue
Macarthur Avenue
Suttor Avenue
Park Road
Bent Street
Wheat Road
Cook Road
Darvall Street
Jervois Avenue
Centennial Road
Parkes Drive (Avenue of Palms)
Desmond Road
Lang Road
Grand Drive
F
G
H

Australian Museum

TOP 25

HIGHLIGHTS

- Aboriginal and Torres Strait collections
- Planet of Minerals room
- Eric
- Australian birds, especially the parrots
- Dinosaurs
- Skeleton Gallery
- Kidspace

TIP

- Ask for a re-entry pass if you'd like to picnic in adjacent Hyde Park.

Rated among the world's top natural history museums, the Australian Museum highlights the country's unique fauna and geology as well as the history of Australia's indigenous people.

The collection Housed in an 1849 building, with more recent additions, the museum has an excellent Aboriginal area, a showcase of native birds, insects and mammals and an informative display on gems and minerals. One of the most interesting sections is the Skeleton Gallery, where the internal organs of various creatures, including a cycling human, can be examined. A must-see permanent exhibition, Dinosaurs brings the prehistoric world of predators and prey imaginatively to life with sounds and smells and even a projection of a dinosaur

Clockwise from top far left: the wonders of nature at the Australian Museum; getting down to the bare bones at the Skeleton Gallery; a lifelike model of ankylosaur Minmi *in the Dinosaurs exhibition; minerals on display in the Chapman Galley; Search and Discover Gallery; facade of the museum; dinosaurs on display*

stampede. And don't miss Eric, a 110- to 120-million-year-old pliosaur; this opalized marine reptile was, incredibly, excavated far inland, at dusty Coober Pedy in South Australia.

Plans for change In June 2014, the NSW government announced a A$7.2 million improvement fund for the museum. Stage one, for completion 2015, sees a new entrance on William Street, new gallery space highlighting biodiversity, and a rooftop brasserie.

Kidspace A museum that educates and intrigues under-5s, featuring five "pods": bugs, marine life, volcanos, observation and imagination. Kids can feel animal skins, solve puzzles and listen to a story. Ask for a free ticket at the admissions desk when you buy your entry ticket.

THE BASICS

australianmuseum.net.au
E7
6 College Street
9320 6000
Daily 9.30–5; closed 25 Dec
Excellent café
Museum
311, 380, 382
Very good
Moderate
Free tours daily; performances, special events and changing exhibitions; museum shop

Art Gallery of New South Wales

Even the statues relax in the grounds (left); pear installation inside the Art Gallery (below)

THE BASICS

www.artgallery.nsw.gov.au
E6
Art Gallery Road, The Domain
9225 1744; free infoline 1 800 679278
Daily 10–5 (Wed 10–10); closed Good Fri, 25 Dec
Excellent restaurant and café
St. James/Martin Place
441 Excellent
Free
Free tours daily, lectures, performances and films; library and shop.

HIGHLIGHTS

- Yiribana Gallery
- Thai bronze Buddhas (Asian Art room)
- Works by Margaret Preston
- Lloyd Rees's paintings
- Photography gallery
- Tom Roberts's paintings

The Aboriginal art is a particularly exciting part of the wonderful collection of Australian, Asian and European art exhibited here. The local works of art offer a wide-ranging view of Australian society and culture.

The collection The original Victorian building has been greatly extended (most recently to mark the 1988 bicentennial) to showcase the gallery's diverse permanent collection and the high-quality visiting international exhibitions. Besides work by European artists and fine Australian painters such as Frederick McCubbin, Arthur Streeton, Margaret Preston, Lloyd Rees, Tom Roberts and Sidney Nolan, the gallery has an excellent Asian art section, whose ceramics are highly rated among connoisseurs. On show are examples of Chinese and Japanese art from ancient times to the present day. The spread of Buddhism is traced in art from India across Asia. European highlights include works by Picasso, Van Gogh, Degas and Rodin. The prints and drawings room and the photography gallery are also well worth visiting.

The Yiribana Gallery The name means "this way" in the language of the Eora people. The gallery contains Australia's most comprehensive collection of Aboriginal and Torres Strait Islander art. More than 200 items, from contemporary paintings to sculptures and traditional works on bark, are housed here, representing artists from communities across Australia. The Yiribana Project Space hosts changing exhibitions.

The lake in Sydney's Centennial Park (below); a purple gallinule or swamp hen (right)

TOP 25

Centennial Park

One of Sydney's largest green spaces, Centennial Park is perfect for picnicking, walking, jogging, cycling, horse riding or rollerblading. The fashionable suburbs of Paddington and Woollahra are nearby.

The park Originally known as Sydney Common and used for grazing animals, Centennial Park is the inner-city's largest expanse of greenery. Although it is relatively crowded on weekends and a hive of activity before and after work hours during the week, Centennial Park is quiet during the day and a good place for a picnic or just relaxing. You can lose yourself among lakes, grassland, woods or the swamp, or spot some of the 200 species of birds that have been recorded seasonally. If you'd like a tour, there are ranger-guided nature and bird walks, or you can rent bicycles, rollerblades and horses to circle the 4km (2.5-mile) Grand Drive. The Federation Pavilion, which was opened in 1988 (Australia's bicentenary year), commemorates the nation's federation ceremony, which took place in the park in 1901.

Paddington and Woollahra These adjoining suburbs (▷ 76) provide much to do, with interesting clothing and antiques shops, excellent cafés, quaint streets and on Saturday the famous Paddington Markets. Woollahra is an Aboriginal word meaning camp or meeting ground. The name was adopted by Daniel Cooper (1821–1902) the first speaker of the legislative assembly of New South Wales when he built Woollahra House in 1856.

THE BASICS

www.centennialparklands.com.au
- H11
- Centennial Park, off Oxford Street, Woollahra
- 9339 6699
- Daily during daylight hours
- Excellent café
- Bondi Junction
- Bondi & Bay Explorer, 378, 380, 382
- Very good
- Free. Ranger-guided walks inexpensive
- Occasional concerts and special events

HIGHLIGHTS

- Federation Pavilion
- Horse riding
- Walks
- Cycling
- Queen Street, Woollahra
- Oxford Street, Paddington
- Paddington Markets (▷ 86)

City Centre

TOP 25

Archibald Fountain in Hyde Park (left); the fountain illuminated at night (below)

THE BASICS

www.cityofsydney.nsw.gov.au
D7
Town Hall tours 9265 9333
Tours daily
Town Hall, Museum
Few
Free

HIGHLIGHTS

- Sydney Town Hall
- Harry Seidler buildings
- Hyde Park
- St. Andrews Cathedral
- Chifley Tower
- Archibald Fountain

TIP

- Join the office workers for a lunchtime sandwich in Hyde Park.

Many of Sydney's colonial-era and Victorian buildings have been lovingly restored and you can walk around the city to view some architectural gems. Don't forget the interesting little backstreets.

Colonial and Victorian Sydney From its origins as a convict settlement, Sydney has always had fine public and commercial buildings that were progressively replaced with grander versions as the years went by and the population rapidly increased. Fortunately, a few colonial buildings, such as the Hyde Park Barracks (▷ 75) and St. James Church, remain, as do examples of 19th-century local sandstone architecture. One such is the Town Hall in George Street, an elaborate 1869 building. You can look at the decorative vestibule and grand hall at any time, or join one of the tours that take place. Next door is St. Andrew's Cathedral (▷ 82), while St. Mary's Cathedral (▷ 82) is on the eastern side of Hyde Park.

Art deco Sydney A number of buildings survive, but the Anzac War Memorial (▷ 79), in the southern part of Hyde Park (▷ 80) and the Archibald Fountain, in the northern section, are the most accessible and classic of all structures from this era.

Modern Sydney While many of the city's modern structures are not architecturally important, some buildings are worth finding: Chifley Tower (▷ 79) at Chifley Square and the Harry Seidler-designed buildings, the MLC Centre in Martin Place and Australia Square in George Street.

Outdoor café (below) at the former detention center, Hyde Park Barracks (right)

TOP 25

Hyde Park Barracks

This building, once home to convicts, was designed by the ex-forger turned architect Francis Greenway. Now a museum, there are remarkable displays covering convict life and Sydney's early years.

The barracks Located on historic Macquarie Street, Hyde Park Barracks (1819) is perhaps the city's most charming building. Standing in dignified seclusion behind its grand gates, this three-floor example of Georgian architecture originally accommodated convicts and later became a home for destitute women. The building is now a fascinating museum, focusing on the lives of these occupants and providing a glimpse into Sydney's early days. Changing exhibitions are mounted on the ground-floor Greenway Gallery. The most enjoyable way to appreciate the simple but elegant building, however, is by stopping for a coffee or meal at the delightful Hyde Park Barracks Café situated in the courtyard.

Queens Square and Macquarie Street The city's finest and most historically significant avenue, Macquarie Street, begins outside the barracks at Queens Square, which is anchored by an 1888 statue of Queen Victoria. This area contains the city's oldest church, the 1822 St. James (another Francis Greenway building), and the 1816 Sydney Mint. To appreciate thoroughly Macquarie Street's charms, walk past Victorian Sydney Hospital, the Sydney Mint and State Parliament House (▷ 81), built in 1816, to the State Library (▷ 81).

THE BASICS

www.sydneylivingmuseums.com.au
E6
Queens Square, Macquarie Street
8239 2311
Daily 10–5; closed Good Fri, 25 Dec
Hyde Park Barracks Café (▷ 90)
Martin Place/St. James
200, 311
Circular Quay
Few
Moderate

HIGHLIGHTS

- Elegant architecture
- Exhibitions in the Greenway Gallery
- Historic Macquarie Street
- St. James Church
- Statue of Queen Victoria

Paddington

TOP 25

HIGHLIGHTS

- Oxford Street
- Victoria Barracks
- Paddington Markets
- Terraced (row) houses
- Specialty shops
- Arthouse cinemas
- Art galleries

TIP

- Make the trip on a Saturday to coincide with the Paddington Markets.

Trendy Paddington, a near city suburb of Victorian-era terraced (row) houses, straddles the eastern thoroughfare of Oxford Street, which is lined with an array of specialty shops.

Paddington's houses With their decorative wrought-iron balconies and fences, these are an architectural gem. Built between the 1840s and the 1890s as middle-class housing, most have been restored to create a charming suburb, listed as a conservation area by the National Trust. Today, art galleries and antiques shops abound and walking is the perfect way to combine sightseeing, shopping and dining.

The suburb Paddington is divided by Oxford Street, which originates at Hyde Park in the

Clockwise from top far left: the delightful terraced (row) houses of Paddington; Oxford Street is great for shopping; capoeira street performers; visitors check out the houses; pictures on sale at the Paddington Markets; wrought-iron railings and pretty gardens are a feature of Paddington's attractive houses

CBD and runs through the gay district in Darlinghurst, through Paddington, to Bondi Junction. On Saturday, Paddington Markets (▷ 86) draws crowds to the specialty shops selling fashion, homewares, books and gifts. Cafés and restaurants cater for the hungry and thirsty, while three cinema complexes show arthouse movies. Nearby is Centennial Park (▷ 73), an idyllic collection of open spaces.

Victoria Barracks This imposing National Trust listed sandstone-block building was constructed by soldiers and convicts in the 1840s as a barracks, and remains a military base today. The 226m (610ft) long facade sits imposingly in front of a large parade ground. Guided tours include the military museum and other sections of the base.

THE BASICS

www.sydney.com
G9
Victoria Barracks, Oxford Street
8335 5330
Tours Thu 10–1. Museum Sun 10–1
Numerous cafés and restaurants
378, 380, 382
Inexpensive; tours free

Sydney Tower and Skywalk

Sydney Tower and other skyscrapers (left); the tower seen from Hyde Park (below)

THE BASICS

www.sydneytowereye.com.au
D7
Level 5, Westfield Sydney Shopping Centre, 100 Market Street
1 800 258693
Daily summer 9am-10pm, winter 9am–9.30pm. Last entry 1 hour before closing. Closed 25 Dec
Revolving restaurants, coffee lounge
St. James/Town Hall
Any bus along George Street or Elizabeth Street
Good
Expensive

HIGHLIGHTS

- View of Sydney Harbour, the city buildings and south to Botany Bay
- Night views
- Revolving restaurants
- High-speed elevator
- Skywalk
- 4-D cinema

This 305m (1,000ft) high structure, soaring dizzily above the city, is the best place to view Sydney's layout. The incredible panorama from the tower's viewing levels extends to the Blue Mountains on a clear day.

The structure Completed in 1981, gold-topped Sydney Tower is anchored by 56 stabilizing cables. One of the tallest public buildings in the southern hemisphere, it contains two revolving restaurants, an observation level, a 4-D cinema and a coffee shop. A ride in one of the three high-speed, double-deck elevators—a journey that takes a mere 40 seconds—is an experience in itself. High-powered binoculars on the enclosed Observation Deck bring highlight sights into close-up view. Zoom in on the Harbour's intricate shoreline, check out some beachside playgrounds and focus in on aviation activity at Sydney's busy airport. Interactive touchscreens offer fast facts and useful information on famous landmarks. The 4-D Cinema Experience encapsulates many facets of the city through engaging film footage and special in-theater effects.

Skywalk Constructed at the top of Sydney Tower in 2005, the A$4million Skywalk is twice the height of the Sydney Harbour Bridge. The 45-minute guided tour around the outside of the Tower's golden turret offers an exciting, bird's-eye view of the city, especially when you look down through the Skywalk's glass-floor viewing platform. A visit after dark is magical.

More to See

ANZAC WAR MEMORIAL

www.anzacmemorial.nsw.gov.au

This huge 1934 art deco structure, decorated with poignant sculptures, is Sydney's tribute to all Australians who served their country in war. Inside, the domed ceiling is dotted with 120,000 stars representing each man and woman from New South Wales who served overseas in World War I.

D7 Hyde Park South 9267 7668 Daily 9–5. Closed Good Fri and 25 Dec Nearby Museum Free

AUSTRALIAN CENTRE FOR PHOTOGRAPHY

www.acp.org.au

Australia's premier photography gallery, established in 1973, has two exhibition spaces, a project wall for emerging artists, a workshop with public access and a specialist bookshop. For interested practitioners there is a darkroom facility, a digital workstation and a research library. The excellent gallery is a nonprofit organization.

G9 257 Oxford Street, Paddington 9332 0555 Tue–Sat 10–5, Sun 12–5. Closed 23 Dec–7 Jan Nearby 3733, 380, 382 Free

BRETT WHITELEY STUDIO

www.artgallery.nsw.gov.au/brett-whiteley-studio

This museum and gallery, opened in 1995, is a tribute to Brett Whiteley, born in 1939, one of Australia's most important and controversial modern artists, who died of a drug overdose in 1993. His studio, now managed by the Art Gallery of NSW (▷ 72), is full of his sculptures, paintings, drawings and memorabilia.

E10 2 Raper Street, Surry Hills 9225 1881 Fri–Sun 10–4 Nearby 302, 372 Free

CHIFLEY TOWER

www.chifley.com.au

Nearly all of Sydney's newer skyscrapers have interesting rooflines. One such is Chifley Tower, built in 1993, which also has some very chic shops and marble and terrazzo walkways inside. Alongside

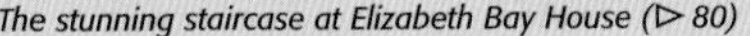

The stunning staircase at Elizabeth Bay House (▷ 80)

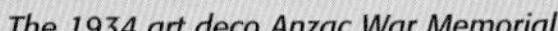

The 1934 art deco Anzac War Memorial

the international and national retailers is an extensive food court, as well as some good restaurants and great Harbour views.
D6 Chifley Square 9221 4500 Daily Cafés and restaurants Martin Place Free

ELIZABETH BAY HOUSE

www.sydneylivingmuseums.com.au
Constructed from Sydney sandstone, the elegant Elizabeth Bay House was built between 1835 and 1839. The house's most important feature is its oval-shaped salon and winding staircase, regarded as Australia's finest. Rooms are open to the public and are furnished in Regency style.
F6 7 Onslow Avenue, Elizabeth Bay 9356 3022 Fri–Sun 11–4 Nearby Kings Cross Inexpensive

HYDE PARK

This CBD haven has been a park since 1810 and is a popular lunchtime spot for city workers. You can wander among formal gardens and tree-lined paths and visit the Anzac War Memorial (▷ 79).
D7 Off Elizabeth Street Daily Nearby St. James Free

KINGS CROSS AND POTTS POINT

Once Sydney's most Bohemian district, Kings Cross is now somewhat seedy, but it's the place for late nightlife. Adjacent Potts Point (Macleay and Victoria streets in particular) has interesting old domestic architecture and cafés.
F8, F7 Many cafés and restaurants Kings Cross Free

QUEEN VICTORIA BUILDING

www.qvb.com.au
The delightfully restored interior of Sydney's most imposing Victorian-era building prompted French fashion guru Pierre Cardin to describe the structure as "the most beautiful shopping center in the world." Constructed to commemorate Queen Victoria's Golden Jubilee, and completed in 1898, the

Chill out at lunchtime in Hyde Park

The illuminated Archibald Fountain, Hyde Park

domed Romanesque-style QVB was originally used to house markets downstairs and offices upstairs.

Capped by a central glass dome, the 200m (180ft) long building, occupying an entire city block and containing more than 180 shops, cafés and restaurants, features beautiful stained-glass windows, patterned floor tiles and period shades and appointments, while the four main floors are divided into elegant Victorian-fronted shops. The lower-level food court and ground-floor shops are more run-of-the-mill, but the upper floors contain outlets for international labels as well as excellent local designers and a wide range of quality souvenir shops. On Victoria Walk (second floor), there is an interesting collection of historical objects. Here you can admire a replica of the British Crown jewels, an incredibly ornate Chinese jade bridal carriage, the extraordinary "Royal Clock" and a jade tree.

D7 Corner of George, York, Market and Druitt streets 9264 9209 Mon–Sat shops generally 9–6 (Thu 9–9), Sun 11–5 Many food stalls, cafés and restaurants Town Hall Any Circular Quay-bound bus Very good Free

STATE LIBRARY OF NEW SOUTH WALES

www.sl.nsw.gov.au

More than just a library, this large complex has a good shop, talks, events, festivals, exhibitions (a small charge for some) and free tours. You can also browse among the vast collection of books and other material on Australia.

E6 Macquarie Street 9273 1414 Mon–Thu 9–8, Fri 9–5, Sat–Sun 10–5. Closed 1 Jan, Good Fri, Easter Sun, 25–26 Dec Licensed café Martin Place Free

STATE PARLIAMENT HOUSE

www.parliament.nsw.gov.au

Originally part of the Rum Hospital, Parliament House (built in 1816) is a fine example of early colonial architecture, and features shady verandas. The building was extended during the 1970s and 1980s to meet the demands of a growing government

Exterior of the Queen Victoria Building

Stained-glass window in the State Library

administration. You can take a tour of the building, but it is advisable to make a reservation.

E6 Macquarie Street Tours 9230 2047 Tours: check website for dates Nearby Martin Place Free

ST. ANDREW'S CATHEDRAL

www.sydneycathedral.com

St. Andrew's, built in the Gothic Revival style and consecrated in 1868, is the mother church of the Anglican Diocese of Sydney. Visitors are welcome to look around inside and to attend services (check website for times).

D7 Corner of George and Bathurst streets 9265 1661 Town Hall Free

ST. MARY'S CATHEDRAL

www.stmaryscathedral.org.au

One of the finest 19th-century Gothic-Revival churches in the world, the church has stunning stained-glass windows and a stunning mosaic tile floor in the crypt. Free guided tours on Sunday at 12, following the Solemn Choral Mass.

E7 Corner of St. Mary's Road and College Street 9220 0400 St. James Free

SYDNEY CRICKET GROUND

www.sydneycricketground.com.au

The famed SCG is the home of first-class cricket in New South Wales. Test and one-day matches are played in summer, or you can visit the stadium and its Cricket Museum on a tour—SGC Tour Experience (1300 724 737).

F10 Driver Avenue, Moore Park 9360 6601 Tours Mon–Fri 11 and 2, Sat 10 371–377, 392–399

WOOLLOOMOOLOO

This glitzy inner-city address, with its Aboriginal name, has some quaint terraced (row) houses. On Cowper Wharf Road you will find the historic Finger Wharf that juts far out into the bay, ships of the Australian Navy's fleet and Artspace, a gallery of contemporary art.

F7 Artspace, 43–51 Cowper Wharf Road 9356 0555 Tue–Fri 11–5, Sat–Sun 12–4 Nearby 311 Free

The neo-Gothic St. Mary's Cathedral

Full house at the Sydney Cricket Ground

Paddington and Woollahra

Walk the backstreets of these two trendy inner-city suburbs to view the interesting architecture and check out the shops.

DISTANCE: 3km (2 miles) **ALLOW:** 45 minutes–2 hours

START

CNR OXFORD AND QUEEN STREETS

 G10 378, 380

❶ Paddington and Woollahra grew up around the 1841 Victoria Barracks (▷ 77) and by the 1880s was crammed with terraced (row) houses. With their iron lacework balconies, the brick-built terraces make Paddington unique and charming.

❷ From the intersection of Oxford Street turn left on to Queen Street, full of exclusive antiques shops. Take a left on to Moncur Street and walk down Hargrave Street.

❸ You are now in the conservation area of Paddington listed by the National Trust. Turn left to Elizabeth Street, right to Paddington Street and right again on to Cascade Street.

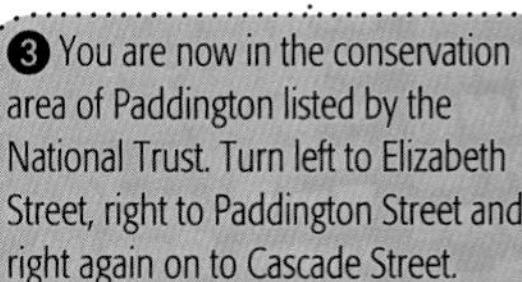

❹ Cascade Street has some particularly good examples of the local architecture, made in the local sandstone material. Walk down Cascade Street and head left on to Gurner Street.

❺ Continue along Glenmore Road to Five Ways.

❻ Approximately 200m (180 yards) farther along Glenmore Road, turn left on to steep Ormond Street. Back on Oxford Street, turn left to reach the main Paddington shopping and café strip.

❼ This is home to Sydney's most interesting clothing shops as well as book, music and jewelry outlets. The Saturday Paddington Markets is held here (▷ 86).

END

OXFORD STREET

G9 378, 380

It also hosts Sydney's oldest theater, the Theatre Royal (▷ 88).
D6 19 Martin Place 9224 8333 Martin Place

THE NUT SHOP

One of Sydney's hidden treasures selling fresh nuts including macadamias, dried fruits and yummy chococate-coated treats. Located in the elegant 19th-century Strand Arcade.
D6 Ground Floor, Strand Arcade 9231 3038 Town Hall

PADDINGTON MARKETS

www.paddingtonmarkets.com.au
This is the trendiest market in town. Mostly clothes, arts, crafts and jewelry at some good prices. The street performers are often very entertaining.
G9 Corner of Oxford and Newcombe streets, Paddington 9331 2923 Sat 10–4 (closes at 4pm in winter) 333,378, 380

PASPALEY PEARLS

www.paspaley.com
Sydney's South Sea pearl specialist, with outlets in Paris, Dubai and New York. Paspaley's northern Australian pearling company is regarded as the source of the finest pearls in the world.
D6 2 Martin Place 9232 7633 Martin Place

PETER SHEPPARD

www.petersheppard.com.au
Specializing in high quality, stylish shoes for women, this store is a dream destination for anyone with narrow, wide or extra wide feet and those that require orthotics. Top European and US brands are stocked for everyday, leisure and special occasion wear.
D6 2 Martin Place 9232 7633 Martin Place

QUEEN VICTORIA BUILDING

www.qvb.com.au
This imposing 1898 building occupies an entire city block and is a delightful environment of stained glass, tiled floors and beautifully appointed shops and cafés (▷ 80).
D7 Corner of George, York, Market and Druitt streets 9264 9209 Town Hall

CHIC SHOPPING

If you're after international designer labels, the best places to visit in the city are Castlereagh Street (names such as Chanel and Louis Vuitton), the MLC Centre, the glossy David Jones Elizabeth Street store and the suburb of Double Bay. Other international stores include Emporio Armani on Martin Place and the Chifley Plaza shops, while you could also splash out on superb jewelry crafted from Australian gold, pearls, opals and diamonds.

R. M. WILLIAMS

www.rmwilliams.com.au
This legendary Bushman's Outfitters sells Australian country and Outback clothing, including moleskin pants, sturdy leather boots and Drizabone oilskin coats. High quality is assured.
D7 4 Westfield Sydney, 188 Pitt Street 9232 6904 St. James Town Hall

THE STRAND ARCADE

www.strandarcade.com.au
This rebuilt historic arcade, originally dating from 1892, contains a number of shops across three levels, surrounded by decorative wrought ironwork and stained-glass windows. There are some good specialty shops, too.
D7 Pitt Street Mall and 412 George Street 9232 4199 St. James

STRAND HATTERS

www.strandhatters.com.au
Bill Clinton has one, Greg Norman plays golf in his and Australian cattlemen wouldn't be seen without one–the genuine Akubra rabbit-skin hat. Strand Hatters can certainly offer the best range of these hats in the city.
D7 Shop 8, Strand Arcade, 412 George Street 9231 6884 Town Hall

Entertainment and Nightlife

ALLIANZ STADIUM

www.allianz.com.au/stadium

Rugby league, rugby union and football (soccer) are played in this ultramodern stadium. You can watch a match during winter, or join one of the guided tours—contact Sportspace Tours (☎ 9380 0383).

✚ F10 ✉ Driver Avenue, Moore Park ☎ 9360 6601 ⌚ Tours Mon–Sat 🚌 372, 373, 377, 393, 394, 396

ARQ

www.arqsydney.com.au

Ultrachic design combined with a variety of dance music. It is best to check the information line as things change regularly at this gay club.

✚ E8 ✉ 16 Flinders Street, Taylor Square ☎ 9380 8700 ⌚ Thu–Sat 9pm–closure varies 🚌 378, 380

BELVOIR STREET THEATRE

www.belvoir.com.au

Company B, a long-established acting company, performs some of Australia's newest productions.

✚ D9 ✉ 25 Belvoir Street, Surry Hills ☎ 9667 3444 🚉 Central

BURDEKIN HOTEL

www.burdekin.com.au

This popular hotel in Darlinghurst has a large bar on the Oxford Street side and the more intimate, expensive art deco Dug Out Bar on Liverpool Street, with its flattering low lighting and friendly, attentive staff.

✚ E8 ✉ 2 Oxford Street, Darlinghurst ☎ 9331 3066 ⌚ Wed–Fri 4pm–late, Sat 6pm–late 🚉 Museum

CENTENNIAL PARK

The perfect venue for cycling, horse riding, walking, rollerblading and jogging. Horses and equipment can be rented (▷ 73). It's also the summer home of the Moonlight Cinema (▷ 88).

✚ H10 ✉ Off Oxford Street, Woollahra ☎ 9339 6699 ⌚ Daily during daylight hours 🚌 378, 380, 382

COOPER PARK TENNIS COURTS

www.cptennis.com.au

Scenically, there is no better place for tennis than this bushland spot between Bondi Junction and Double Bay.

✚ J9 ✉ 1 Bunna Place, off Suttie Road, Woollahra ☎ 9389 9259 ⌚ Daily 🚉 Bondi Junction, then bus 330

GAY AND LESBIAN

Sydney is the home of the world's largest gay and lesbian parade—the Mardi Gras—that takes place each February or March. The area around lower Oxford Street (sometimes referred to as the Great Gay Way) is the heart of this alternative scene. Many hotels, bars and clubs here cater to the LGBT community; popular venues include the Midnight Shift (▷ 88), the Lord Roberts Hotel (✉ 64 Stanley Street, East Sydney) and the Newtown Hotel (✉ 174 King Street, Newtown).

DOWNTOWN

www.thecommons.com.au

The downstairs bar at The Commons pub/restaurant is in a great old sandstone building. The bar menu and music are inspired by the golden age of cocktails, jazz and blues.

✚ E8 ✉ 32 Burton Street, Darlinghurst ☎ 9358 1487 ⌚ Wed–Thu 6pm–midnight, Fri–Sat 6pm–1am, Sun 4–11pm. Live jazz Wed, Thu, Sat 🚌 380, 382

ENTERTAINMENT QUARTER

www.eqmoorepark.com.au

This complex of cinemas, restaurants, shops and markets is Sydney's latest entertainment and dining hotspot. There are numerous activities to keep children occupied, such as Equipment at Monkey Mania, an indoor play center.

✚ F10 ✉ Lang Road, Moore Park ☎ 8117 6700 ⌚ Daily 10am–late. Closed 25 Dec 🚌 372, 377, 390, 399

LORD DUDLEY

www.lorddudley.com.au

A very popular English-style pub that (unusually for Sydney) serves beer in pint as well as half-pint

tankards. It has 18 local and imported beers on tap, shows sporting events on large screens and boasts open fires in the lounge in winter. The downstairs eating area serves Modern Australian food with a British twist.
H9 ✉ 236 Jersey Road, Woollahra ☎ 9327 5399 Daily 389

THE METRO

www.metrotheatre.com.au
This is Sydney's leading independent rock venue and is a great place to catch a live band. Dance, comedy, fringe and other performances also feature from time to time. Check out The Lair downstairs, decked out with retro video games, lounges, dance floor and bar, that hosts different types of music, comedy nights and other live performances.
D8 ✉ 624 George Street ☎ 9287 2000 for performance information Town Hall

MIDNIGHT SHIFT

www.themidnightshift.com.au
One of Sydney's most popular gay bars and discos with multi-award-winning entertainment, production shows and top DJs. This is a great place to visit if the gay scene interests you (▷ panel, 87).
E8 ✉ 85 Oxford Street, Darlinghurst ☎ 9358 3848 Wed–Sun 2pm–very late Museum

MOONLIGHT CINEMA

www.moonlight.com.au
Open-air cinema that screens previews, contemporary cult and classic movies on Centennial Park's Belvedere Amphitheatre lawns in summer. Screenings start at sundown (around 8.30pm). Arrive early (from 7pm) to grab one of the bean beds available for hire.
H10 ✉ Nearest gates, Woollahra Gates on Oxford Street, Paddington ☎ See website for ticket and performance information Tue–Sun 7–11pm 378, 380, 382

MOORE PARK GOLF CLUB

www.mooreparkgolf.com.au
Easily accessible from the city, this club offers an 18-hole course, a 60-bay, all weather day and night driving range, and all facilities at very reasonable rates.
F11 ✉ Cleveland Street, Moore Park ☎ 9663 1064 Daily (driving range Mon 10–10, Tue–Thu 6am–midnight, Fri–Sun 6am–10pm) 373, 374, 377, 394

ABORIGINAL DANCE

Bangarra Dance Company, which fuses contemporary and traditional dance routines into dramatic and exciting performances, can be seen at the Theatre Royal and the Opera House (☎ 9251 5333 for details).

ROYAL HOTEL

www.royalhotel.com.au
This charming hotel, set in an old part of Paddington, is known for its upstairs Elephant Bar, which has a great cocktail menu and comfy couches. The restaurant serves bistro meals; get there early for balcony dining in summer.
G9 ✉ 257 Glenmore Road, Five Ways, Paddington ☎ 9331 2604 Mon–Sat 12–12, Sun 12–10 389

STATE THEATRE

www.statetheatre.com.au
This ornate 2,000-seat arena is the venue for musicals, ballet, the Sydney Film Festival and performances of live music. The State dates from 1929 and is National Trust classified because of its splendid art deco interior. There are two-hour tours on Mon, Tue and Wed at 10am and 1pm.
D6 ✉ 49 Market Street ☎ 136 100 to book tours and for performance information Town Hall

THEATRE ROYAL

www.theatreroyal.net.au
This modern central performance venue specializes in putting on long-running musicals but also stages internationally-renowned plays and ballet companies.
D6 ✉ MLC Centre, King Street ☎ 1300 723038 for performance information Martin Place

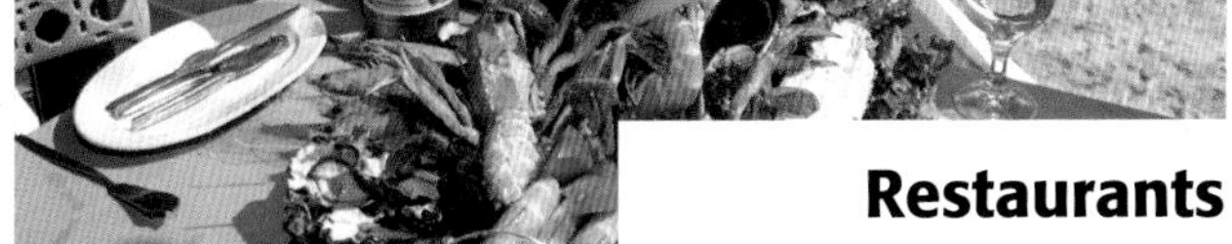

Restaurants

PRICES

Prices are approximate, based on a 3-course meal for one person.
$$$ over A$60
$$ A$40–A$60
$ under A$40

BALKAN SEAFOOD ($$)

www.balkanseafood.com.au
Chargrilled octopus and fish at sensible prices. The Sunday specials are a treat. Although famed for seafood, meat-lovers also have a good choice on the menu, which includes pasta dishes. BYO.
E8 217 Oxford Street, Darlinghurst 9331 2778 Daily 11.30am–late 380

BAR COLUZZI ($)

This tiny café, with its alfresco seating, is deservedly popular. The coffee is some of the best around.
E8 322 Victoria Street, Darlinghurst 9380 5420 Daily 6am–8pm Kings Cross

BILLS ($)

www.bills.com.au
A popular breakfast and lunch spot for those on the run. Long famous for the best scrambled eggs and ricotta hotcakes in town, visitors and locals gather around the communal table, contributing to the buzzy atmosphere.
E8 433 Liverpool Street, Darlinghurst 1360 9631 Daily breakfast, lunch Museum

BISTRODE CBD ($$$)

www.merivale.com.au/bistrocbd
Modern bistro cuisine from the award-winning British chef Jeremy Strode. Menus change daily with seasonal specials. The pub food downstairs is good, too.
D8 Level 1, CBD Hotel, Cnr York and Kings Street 9240 3000 Mon–Fri lunch and dinner, Sat dinner only Wynyard 389

BISTRO MONCUR ($$–$$$)

www.woollahrahotel.com.au
Highly rated, innovative food in a trendy eastern suburbs pub. It can be a bit noisy.
H9 Woollahra Hotel, 116 Queen Street, Woollahra 9327 9713 Thu–Sun lunch, daily dinner 389

EATING OUT IN SYDNEY

Sydney restaurants range from super-inexpensive to the totally indulgent, while cuisines from all over the world are represented. Australian wines are a good accompaniment to meals and many restaurants are BYO (bring your own alcohol)—a small corkage fee is usually charged. Reserving is generally recommended, but some brasserie-style places do not accept reservations. Smoking is banned in cafés, estaurants and in the dining section of pubs and clubs.

CAPITAN TORRES ($$)

www.capitantorres.com.au
A popular central establishment with great Spanish dishes, sangria and a lively atmosphere.
D8 73 Liverpool Street 9264 5574 Daily lunch, dinner Town Hall

CIVIC BISTRO ($)

www.civichotel.com.au
This classic art deco pub features a hip cocktail bar and a range of Modern Australian dishes and tasty desserts.
D8 Corner of Pitt and Goulburn streets 8080 7000 Mon–Sat lunch and dinner Town Hall

FLAVOUR OF INDIA ($$)

www.flavourofindia.co
Sydney isn't renowned for its Indian food, but this is one of the best. In business for 20 years, the dishes span cooking styles from all over the Indian sub-continent.
H8 128 New South Head Road, Edgecliff 9326 2659 Daily dinner Edgecliff

GUSTO ($$)

Hearty breakfasts and a deli lunch special including the works are what makes this café/deli so popular.
G9 2a Healy Street, Paddington 9361 5640

Daily breakfast, lunch and dinner 389

HYDE PARK BARRACKS CAFÉ ($$)

www.hydeparkbarrackscafe.com.au
The menu reveals an array of imaginative dishes and desserts. Eat inside or in the courtyard at this café, which incorporates the original convict confinement area.
D6 Queens Square, Macquarie Street 9222 1815 Mon–Fri 8–3, Sat–Sun 9–3 Martin Place

IPPUDO ($–$$)

www.ippudo.com.au
Popular eatery famed for high-quality, authentic *ramen* and melting pork buns. Lines can be long, but the bar serves Japanese craft beers while you wait.
D7 Level 5, Westfield Sydney, 188 Pitt Street 8078 7020 Mon–Wed 11–10, Thu–Sat 11–11, Sun 11–9 Town Hall

LONGRAIN ($$$)

www.longrain.com/sydney
Long-shared tables and delicious South East Asian-inspired food.
D9 85 Commonwealth Street, Surry Hills 9280 2888 Mon–Fri lunch, dinner daily 378

LUCIO'S ($$$)

www.lucios.com
Top service and top Italian dishes are the trademark of this long-established restaurant. Seasonal ingredients are the order of the day.
G9 47 Windsor Street, Paddington 9380 5996 Tue–Sat lunch, dinner 389

PAVILION ON THE PARK ($$$)

www.pavilionrestaurant.com.au
Enjoy lunch on the delightful terrace with quintessential Sydney vistas. Popular for its good selection of seafood dishes but try the roast lamb loin. The Pavilion Kiosk serves light meals, gourmet sandwiches, muffins and cakes to go or eat on the leafy deck with park views.
E6 1 Art Gallery Road, The Domain 9232 1322 Sun–Fri lunch. Kiosk Sat–Wed 8–4, Thu–Fri 8–7 St. James/Martin Place

ASIAN RESTAURANTS

Multiculturalism has laid the foundation for an array of Asian restaurants in Sydney. The eating places listed here, from Chinese to Indonesian, are just a sample, but you will also find Singaporean, Nepalese, Burmese, Taiwanese, Javanese, Korean and Laotian. Most Asian restaurants are reasonably priced and many are BYO.

SYDNEY TOWER 360 ($$$)

www.360dining.com.au
Fine dining in an elegant setting right in the heart of the CBD, with ever-changing views of the city. The revolving 360 Bar & Dining at the top of the Sydney Tower has dramatic decor and the skills of an award-winning head chef. There's a less expensive, family-friendly buffet restaurant atop the Tower, too.
D7 Gallery Level 4, 4 Sydney Westfield Centre, Cnr Market Street and Pitt Street Mall 8223 3800 Daily lunch, dinner Town Hall

TETSUYA'S ($$$)

www.tetsuyas.com.au
Japanese cuisine transformed to an Australian artform by one of Sydney's top chefs. As winner of several prestigious awards, reservations at this restaurant are essential.
C8 529 Kent Street 9267 2900 Sat lunch, Tue–Sat dinner Town Hall 438

TUM TUM'S THAI TAKEAWAY ($)

This very popular, bustling take-out establishment also has a small eating-in area. It produces fresh, delicious food. Also a BYO—if you can find a seat.
E8 199 Darlinghurst Road, Darlinghurst 9331 5390 Daily noon–11 Kings Cross

Relax at the coastal holiday suburbs of Manly and Bondi or go for sports action at Olympic Park. Also on offer are day-trips to the nearby dramatic Blue Mountains, or a wine-tasting trip to the famed Hunter Valley.

Hunter Valley
HORNSBY
KU-RING-GAI
CASTLE HILL
Koala Park Sanctuary
Pennant Hills Park
GORDON
Excelsior Park
Hawkesbury Valley
Lane Cove
PARRAMATTA
LANE COVE
RYDE
Parramatta
HUNTERS HILL
Sydney Olympic Park
DRUMMOYNE
CONCORD
AUBURN
STRATHFIELD
BURWOOD
LEICHHARDT
MARRICKVILLE
BANKSTOWN
CANTERBURY
Blue Mountains
HURSTVILLE
Southern Highlands, Southern National Parks
ROCKDALE
Sydney Airport
Botany Bay

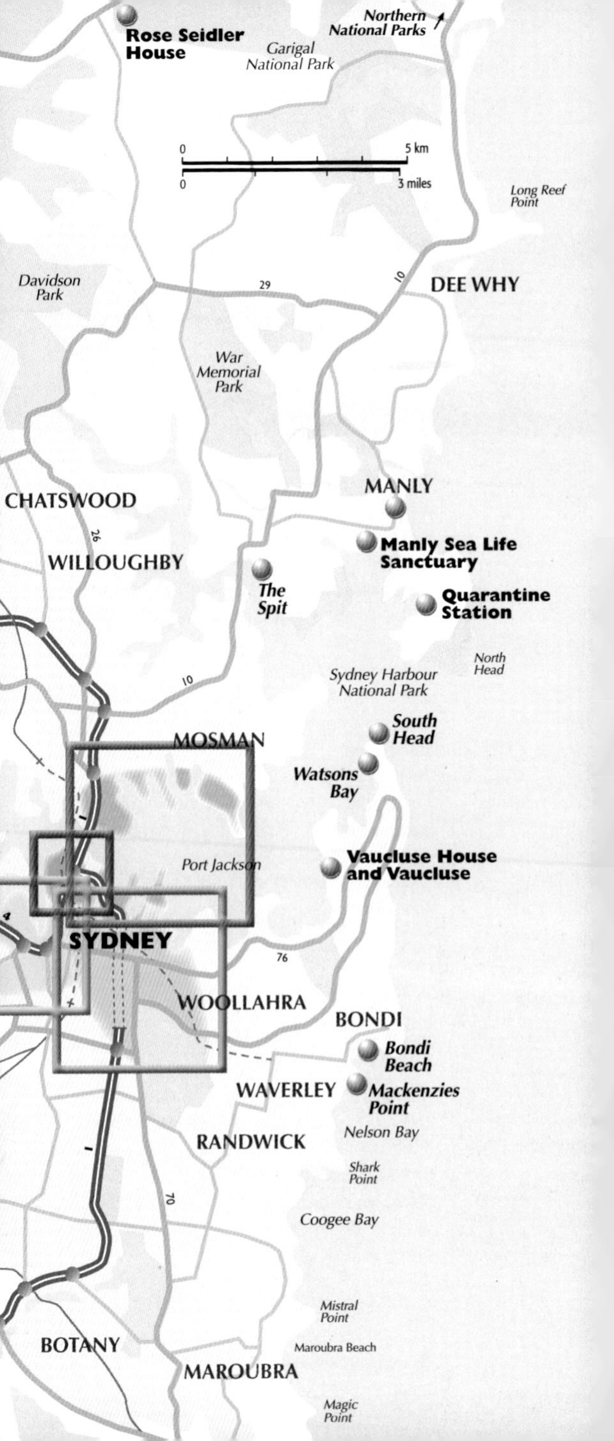
Rose Seidler House
Northern National Parks
Garigal National Park
0
5 km
0
3 miles
Long Reef Point
Davidson Park
29
10
DEE WHY
War Memorial Park
CHATSWOOD
MANLY
26
Manly Sea Life Sanctuary
WILLOUGHBY
The Spit
Quarantine Station
North Head
Sydney Harbour National Park
10
South Head
MOSMAN
Watsons Bay
Port Jackson
Vaucluse House and Vaucluse
4
SYDNEY
76
WOOLLAHRA
BONDI
Bondi Beach
WAVERLEY
Mackenzies Point
Nelson Bay
RANDWICK
Shark Point
70
Coogee Bay
Mistral Point
BOTANY
Maroubra Beach
MAROUBRA
Magic Point

Bondi Beach

TOP 25

One of the world's most famous surfing beaches, Bondi, should not be missed

THE BASICS

www.bondivillage.com
See map ▷ 92–93
Bondi Beach
Bondi Pavilion Community Cultural Centre 8362 3400
Daily 24 hours
Cafés and restaurants
Bondi Junction, then bus 380, 382
Bondi & Bay Explorer, 380, 382, 389
Generally good
Free
Frequent festivals, exhibitions and events

HIGHLIGHTS

- Beach
- Cafés on Campbell Parade
- Exhibitions and events in Bondi Pavilion Community Cultural Centre
- Clifftop walk to Bronte Beach
- Golf overlooking the ocean
- Surfing
- Bondi Markets

Enjoy Sydney's outdoor life at this world-famous strip of surf and sand. Regardless of the season, join the locals as they swim, sunbathe, jog, eat, drink or simply stroll along the water's edge. This is the place for people-watching.

Bondi Beach Summer or winter, Bondi is quintessential Sydney. This is one of the world's most famous strips of surf, sand and beach life, and there is no better way of understanding how the locals enjoy themselves than to head down to Bondi. The Aboriginal name roughly means "the noise of tumbling waters", a description that aptly sums up this beach and its rolling surf. Perfect for a summer sunbathing and surfing session, or a brisk winter walk along the clifftop path to Tamarama and Bronte beaches. Bondi is Sydney at its very best. In summer you may see a surf carnival or other beach event, while the Bondi Pavilion Community Cultural Centre often holds musical and theatrical performances and art exhibitions.

Beachside Bondi street life is just as entertaining, with its bars, pubs and cafés, as well as a good bookshop and surf and beach clothing shops. You can even play golf overlooking the ocean at the public Bondi Golf Course. Bondi is also a great place to stay, with a growing range of accommodations to suit all budgets. Every Sunday (10–5), the grounds of Bondi Beach Public School become the Bondi Markets (▷ 104), and here you'll find designer clothing, handmade jewelry, arts, crafts, homewares and secondhand goods.

The ultimate chill-out destination—Manly is a top weekend spot for Sydneysiders

Manly and Manly Sea Life Sanctuary

The slogan "seven miles from Sydney and a thousand miles from care" originated in the late 1880s, when ferries greatly shortened the journey to the popular suburb of Manly. Sydneysiders have flocked here ever since.

Manly The ocean beach at Manly is a spectacular setting for annual sporting events such as Ironman competitions, bicycle races, surf life-saving carnivals, as well as beach volleyball and swimming tournaments. In summer, Manly and its excellent beaches such as Shelly—all just a short ferry ride from the city—draw surfers and swimmers, but there is plenty to do here at any time. The Manly Art Gallery and Museum has a good collection, and you can stroll around the modern Manly Wharf, with more than 65 shops and cafés, as well as watch free street-entertainment. Continue to North Head and visit the historic Quarantine Station, or take a bus excursion to the wonderful northern beaches, such as Palm Beach or Mona Vale.

Crafty The Manly Arts and Crafts Market (Sat and Sun 9–5), at the lower end of Sydney Road adjacent to the Corso, is worth a look. Check out the variety of quality work from local artists.

Manly Sea Life Sanctuary This big aquarium features vibrant fish of the Great Barrier Reef, as well as corals, sharks, giant stingrays and seal shows. The sharks are hand-fed twice a day and there's Shark Dive Xtreme (▷ 105) for the brave.

THE BASICS

www.manlyaustralia.com.au
www.manlysealifesanctuary.com.au

See map ▷ 92–93

Oceanworld, West Esplanade, Manly

Manly Sea Life Sanctuary 1800 199 742

Daily 10–5.30. Closed 25 Dec

Manly Few

Manly Sea Life Sanctuary expensive

Guided tours, special aquarium shows and events

HIGHLIGHTS

Manly:

- Main beach and Shelly Beach
- Weekend Arts and Crafts Market
- Manly Art Gallery and Museum

Manly Sea Life Sanctuary:

- Great Barrier Reef display
- Seal shows
- Stingrays
- Divers hand-feeding sharks

Sydney Olympic Park

TOP 25

HIGHLIGHTS

- Sydney Aquatic Centre
- Telstra Stadium
- NSW Hall of Champions
- Bicentennial Park

TIP

- Reserve your sports activities in advance.

After hosting the "best Olympics ever", Sydneysiders have embraced the Games site. But you will find more than Olympic memories here as you can participate in a sport of your choice.

Learn about sport The massive facility built for the Sydney 2000 Olympic Games has been transformed into a focus site for entertainment and sport. The best way to get here is by RiverCat ferry from Circular Quay. ANZ Stadium, the site of the Olympic opening and closing ceremonies and focal point of the Sydney Olympic Park, now hosts major rugby and football (soccer) games. Guided tours run daily. The NSW Hall of Champions features photographs and memorabilia of athletes from the 1890s to the present. ANZ Stadium, in the Sydney Olympic

Clockwise from top far left: a participating athlete at the Australian Youth Olympics, Olympic Park; the Olympic swimming pool, on the north side of the bridge; on target at Sydney International Archery Park; high jump at the Youth Olympics; on the race track; ready for hockey at the Homebush Bay Olympic Complex

Park, is the largest multi-use live entertainment and indoor sports arena in Australia.

Play sport Sydney Aquatic Centre has four world-class swimming pools. The complex also has spas, a sauna and steam room, a gym plus a children's water playground, high ropes adventure course and a café. The Sydney International Tennis Centre has courts for rent and offers individual coaching. As well as offering various ball games, the Sydney Indoor Sports Centre also hosts concerts and exhibitions.

Bicentenial Park This green space comprises 40ha (99 acres) of parklands set in an important wetland ecosystem. Facilities include barbecues, picnic shelters, trails, play areas, bicycle paths and an information point.

THE BASICS

www.sydneyolympicpark.com.au
See map ▷ 92–93
Homebush Bay
Park & ANZ Stadium 9714 7888.
NSW Hall of Champions & Sydney Showground 9763 0111.
Allphones Arena 8765 4321.
Bicentennial Park 9714 7888
Park daily 24 hours. ANZ Stadium daily 9.30–5.30.
NSW Hall of Champions daily 9–5.
Bicentennial Park daily 6.30am–dusk
Various
Circular Quay/Central Station
Circular Quay
Excellent
Park free; other attractions prices vary
Guided tours available

Vaucluse House and Vaucluse

HIGHLIGHTS

- The architecture
- Kitchen, drawing room and gardens
- Nielsen Park's beach and foreshore walk
- Parsley Bay

TIP

- Combine a trip to Vaucluse House with a seafood lunch at Doyles (▷ 106).

Visit this charming old eastern suburbs waterside mansion to have a look at its distinctive architecture, its interior furnishings, and to enjoy the well-tended gardens and art deco tearooms.

The house and grounds Much of modern-day Vaucluse, one of Sydney's most desirable waterside suburbs, was once part of the large estate of William Charles Wentworth. Set in 11ha (27 acres) of grounds, most of Gothic-style Vaucluse House was constructed in the 1830s for Wentworth, a prominent citizen, barrister and explorer (one of the first men to cross the Blue Mountains in 1813) and the father of the Australian Constitution. The house contains 15 rooms, furnished in the style of the mid-19th century, including an impressive entertaining suite

Clockwise from top left: the castellated Vaucluse House; interior staircase in the house; copper pans in the kitchen; the elaborate drawing room; the house and gardens

as well as a particularly well-presented kitchen. The large drawing room is splendid, with opulent fabrics and furnishings and a bay window that is framed by the shady veranda. Look out for the unusual corridor bedroom on the first floor—it is partitioned off from the hallway by a screen of cupboards. Little remains of the original estate, but the gardens and tearooms are delightful.

The best of Vaucluse This expensive suburb is full of large homes, leafy streets and waterside spots. Parsley Bay is a popular family beach, while the sand and gardens at Shark Beach and Nielsen Park are packed in summer. This latter beach is within Sydney Harbour National Park (▷ 28–29) and was once part of the Vaucluse House estate. You can take a scenic walk, with great views, around the foreshore.

THE BASICS

www.sydneylivingmuseums.com.au

See map ▷ 92–93

Vaucluse House, Wentworth Road, Vaucluse

9388 7922

Fri–Sun 11–4; daily during NSW public hols. Closed Good Fri, 25 Dec

Tearooms 325

Watsons Bay (then bus 325)

Inexpensive

Tours and special events in the gardens

More to See

HUNTERS HILL

An attractive suburb worth visiting for the ferry ride west of the Harbour Bridge and for a look at 1871 Vienna Cottage. This fine example of a small stone tradesman's house also has a small museum. Hunters Hill is a designated conservation area.

See map ▷ 92–93 Vienna Cottage, 38 Alexandra Street 9816 1794 Museum 2nd and 4th Sun 2–4 Hunters Hill Free. Vienna Cottage inexpensive

KOALA PARK SANCTUARY

www.koalapark.com.au

In this private koala sanctuary, in operation since 1930, you can cuddle koalas, hand-feed kangaroos and see traditional bush activities such as sheep shearing and boomerang throwing. Check out the birds, including rainbow lorikeets.

See map ▷ 92–93 84 Castle Hill Road, West Pennant Hills 9484 3141 Daily 9–5. Closed 25 Dec Kiosk and picnic/barbecue area Pennant Hills, then buses 651–5 Expensive

MACKENZIES POINT

The wonderful views from this promontory extend to the beach at Bondi, out to the Pacific Ocean, and south down the rugged coastline.

See map ▷ 92–93 South of Bondi Beach 24 hours 380, 382 Free

NORTHERN NATIONAL PARKS

www.nationalparks.nsw.gov.au

The greater Sydney region contains 10 national parks, as well as other natural reserves. In the north you can visit Cattai, Lane Cove, Garigal and magnificent Ku-ring-gai Chase, but you need to have your own vehicle or take a tour to fully appreciate these superb wilderness areas.

Off map to north 9995 6500 Daily Kiosks and picnic areas Inexpensive

QUARANTINE STATION

www.qstation.com.au

Used since the 1830s to protect Sydney from smallpox, bubonic plague and other contagious diseases by quarantining migrants, the station is now an unusual museum.

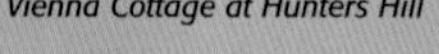

Vienna Cottage at Hunters Hill

A resident of the Koala Park Sanctuary

You can see the burial grounds and rock engravings, while spooky night-time ghost tours come complete with tales of strange happenings.
See map ▷ 92–93 North Head, Manly 9466 1551 Tours daily Manly, then bus 135 Inexpensive

ROSE SEIDLER HOUSE

www. sydneylivingmuseums.com.au
Completed in 1950, this modernist house was designed by Australia's leading architect, Harry Seidler. Its original furniture comprises one of the most important post-war design collections in Australia.
See map ▷ 92–93 71 Clissold Road, Wahnoonnga 9989 8020 Sun 10–4 Turramurra, then bus 575 to Cherrybrook Avenue Inexpensive

SOUTHERN NATIONAL PARKS

www.nationalparks.nsw.gov.au
The city's southern national parks—Kamay Botany Bay, the Royal, Georges River, Thirlmere Lakes and Heathcote—offer scenery ranging from freshwater lakes to beaches. Your own transport is necessary, or contact Allambie Mini Buses.
See map ▷ 92–93 9542 0666 Daily Kiosks and picnic areas Inexpensive

SPIT TO MANLY WALK

This 8km (5-mile) harborside walk takes three to four hours and passes through bushland and the waterfront suburbs surrounding Manly—great views of the Harbour and city.
See map ▷ 92–93 From the Spit Bridge, Middle Harbour 9247 5033 At Manly 178, 180, 182, 190 Free

WATSONS BAY AND SOUTH HEAD

Watsons Bay was once a fishing hamlet and military base. Today, this charming suburb has retained its village atmosphere. There are views of the water, swimming at Camp Cove and a walk to South Head in Sydney Harbour National Park.
See map ▷ 92–93 9337 5511 Daily Cafés and restaurants 324, 325 Watsons Bay Free

Take in the view on the walk to Manly

Excursions

THE BASICS

www.visitbluemountains.com.au

Distance: 58km (36 miles) from Sydney to Katoomba

From Central Station, approximately 2 hours

Blue Mountains Visitor Centres: Glenbrook Tourist Information Centre, Great Western Highway, Glenbrook 1300 653 408; Katoomba Tourist Information Centre, Echo Point Road, Katoomba 1300 653 408; Blue Mountain Heritage Centre, Govetts Leap Road, Blackheath 4787 8877

BLUE MOUNTAINS

Sydneysiders, who have been flocking to the Blue Mountains since the early 19th century, come in summer for the cool mountain air, and in winter for bracing walks and the fireside ambience of the guesthouses.

Cooler than Sydney in summer and bracingly cold in winter, the Blue Mountains are famous for their good hotels, excellent restaurants and grand scenery. People flock to mountain towns like Springwood, Leura, Katoomba, Wentworth Falls, Blackheath and Mt. Victoria to take in the views, walk the trails, shop for arts, crafts and antiques and generally enjoy the mountain air. A variety of superb temperate climate gardens are open for inspection, and the cool-climate annex of the Royal Botanic Gardens at Mt. Tomah is brilliantly hued in the fall and a mass of flowers in the spring and summer.

THE BASICS

www.thehawkesburyaustralia.com.au

Distance: 65km (40 miles)

Journey Time: About an hour's drive northwest of the CBD

Sydney Hills Visitor Information Centre 1300 844 881

HAWKESBURY VALLEY

Visit the quiet hamlets and farms of the Hawkesbury Valley, or cruise the river on a ferry and learn about the region's convict past while you take in the stunning riverside bushland.

The food bowl and timber source for the young colony of Sydney in the 1790s, the Hawkesbury Valley remains today a place of calm and beauty at the city's doorstep. More than 80 percent of the valley is a national park, and there is a rich colonial legacy of old architecture to inspect.

The Hawkesbury River is navigable from the historic town of Windsor to the charming riverside settlement of Brooklyn. Boat tours run from Windsor and Wisemans Ferry, or you can take a trip with the river postman on his weekday run. If you have more time, consider houseboat hire for a few days of idyllic river cruising.

HUNTER VALLEY

Wine lovers make a pilgrimage to this fertile valley, just a couple of hours north from the CBD, to sample new vintages, enjoy country hospitality and relish a memorable dining experience in rural surroundings.

Wine lovers enjoy the trip to the historic Hunter Valley vineyards, three hours north of Sydney, near the old coal mining town of Cessnock. A good selection of bus tours is available from Sydney and, given the nature of the main activity here, may be the preferred means of travel. A well-established circuit travels past the cellar doors of dozens of wineries, where you are encouraged to sample the different products and may be invited to meet and observe the winemakers in their cellars. There are many fine restaurants in the area where you can buy a good meal accompanied by some excellent local wines.

THE BASICS

www.winecountry.com.au
Distance: 120km (72 miles)
Journey Time: Bus trip takes 3 hours
Bus from Sydney
Hunter Valley Tourist Information 455 Wine Country Drive, Pokolbin, near Cessnock
4994 6700

SOUTHERN HIGHLANDS

Rural towns and villages with old-world charm, specialty shops, country estates with grand gardens, and cosy B&Bs set in pretty surroundings are all good reasons to head for the Southern Highlands.

Unwind in the Southern Highlands, a couple of hours' easy driving to the southwest of the city. The hospitality ranges from grand manors to small B&Bs, and the tariff often includes a hearty breakfast based on fresh produce. Arts and crafts outlets, antiques shops, bookshops and specialist food outlets are found in the charming towns and villages, with top restaurants for fine dining.

Mittagong is the regional retail hub, but the nearby town of Berrima has Australia's best-preserved Georgian architecture. Cricket fans can visit the Bradman Museum in Bowral, while lovers of English garden styles will find plenty of choices.

THE BASICS

www.southern-highlands.com.au
Distance: 130km (81 miles)
Journey Time: Two hours' drive southwest of the CBD
Southern Highlands and Mittagong Visitor Information Centre
1300 657 559/4871 2888

Shopping

THE AUSTRALIAN GEOGRAPHIC SHOP

Operated by a popular magazine, this shop sells unusual and environmentally friendly Australian books, gifts and sturdy outdoor clothing.

Off map ✉ Shop 1001, Westfield Shopping Centre, Bondi Junction ☎ 9257 0060 Bondi Junction

BERRIMA VILLAGE POTTERY

www.berrimavillagepottery.com.au

Sells a large range of functional and decorative pottery that is made on site, as well as beautiful homewares from around the world.

Off map ✉ 8 Jellore Street, Berrima ☎ 4877 1987

BLUE MOUNTAINS CHOCOLATE COMPANY

www.bluemountainschocolate.com.au

Watch chocolate being made, take part in a chocolate-making course, enjoy free tastings, and choose from 60 different handmade chocolates.

Off map ✉ 176 Lurline Street, Katoomba ☎ 4782 7071 Katoomba

BONDI MARKETS

www.bondimarkets.com.au

Every Sunday, stalls at this beachfront market fill up with arts, crafts, designer clothing, retro furniture and an interesting range of pre-owned goods.

Off map ✉ Corner of Campbell Parade and Warners Avenue, Bondi Beach ☎ 9315 8988 Sun 10–4; Farmers' Market Sat 9–1 380, 382

BONDI SURF CO.

www.bondisurfco.net.au

Everything for the surfer. You can rent surfboards and boogie boards to try out in the Bondi surf and buy beachwear, including the popular Billabong, Rip Curl and Hot Tuna brands.

Off map ✉ Shop 2, 80 Campbell Parade, Bondi Beach ☎ 9365 0870 380, 382

AUSTRALIAN DELICACIES

While in Sydney, make sure you sample some classic Australian delicacies. Cheeses, particularly those that are made in Tasmania, are wonderful—try King Island cheddar and camembert. Seafood is relatively inexpensive to buy and incredibly varied—choose from everything from Sydney rock oysters to Tasmanian smoked salmon—and most fish shops will cook your selection. Typically Australian-grown fruits and vegetables such as mangoes, bananas, avocados and pineapples are plentiful and available in most food outlets. Other Australian specialties to try are macadamia nuts, Tasmanian honey and, of course, wines.

THE BROOK

www.bluemountainsattractions.com.au/brook-art-a-crafts-co-op.html

Everything herehas been handcrafted by local artists—prints, paintings, patchwork, jewelry, cards, soaps, stained glass and wooden toys. A cooperative business staffed by its crafter members.

Off map ✉ 1a Ross Street, Glenbrook, Blue Mountains ☎ 4739 9511

PARIS CAKE SHOP

www.pariscakeshop.com.au

Wonderfully fresh cakes and pastries, including French specialties such as *brioche, pain au chocolat* and croissants.

Off map ✉ 91 Bondi Road, Bondi ☎ 9387 2496 380, 382

RIP CURL SURF SHOP

www.ripcurl.com.au

This iconic surf label provides everything you need to wear for a great day surfing or just for hanging out, plus surfboards and all the latest gear.

Off map ✉ 82 Campbell Parade, Bondi Beach ☎ 9130 2660 380, 382

TUCHUZY

www.tuchuzy.com

Ultra-chic designer fashion boutique with stylish imports and the best of Australian talent.

Off map ✉ Shop 11, The Beach House, 178 Campbell Parade, Bondi Beach ☎ 9365 7775 380, 381, 382

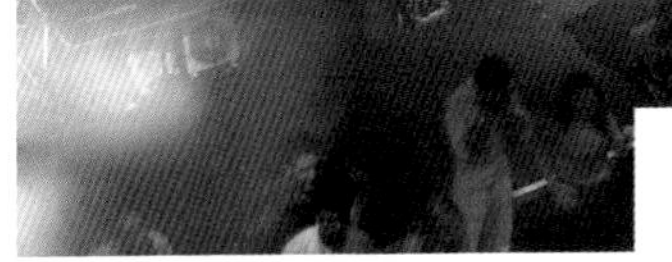

Entertainment and Nightlife

AUSTRALIAN REPTILE PARK

www.reptilepark.com.au

Located at Gosford on the Central Coast less than an hour's drive north of Sydney. On show are reptiles of all kinds, including crocodiles, snakes and the wonderful Galapagos tortoises, which can weigh up to 180kg (400lb) and live for as long as 160 years. Also koalas, kangaroos, emus and parrots and Australia's only spider zoo, featuring Spider World and Tarantulaville—not for the fainthearted.

Off map · Pacific Highway, Somersby · 4340 1022 · Daily 9–5

CITY FARM CALMSLEY HILL

www.calmsleyhill.com.au

This is a great place for the family to share some experiences of bush life, including shearing sheep, tractor rides and milking demonstrations. Café, milk-bar style take-out and lots of space to picnic—at tables or on the grass.

Off map · 31 Darling Street, Abbotsbury · 9823 3222 · Daily 9–4.30 · Fairfield

CLOUD 9 BALLOON FLIGHTS

www.cloud9balloons.com.au

An adventurous way to view Sydney is from the air. Take a hot-air balloon flight and follow it with a champagne breakfast.

Off map · Annangrove · 1300 555 711 · Daily at dawn · Parramatta

HOTEL BONDI

www.hotelbondi.com.au

After a day on the beach this is a great place to mix with the locals, listen to live bands, play pool or just hang out.

Off map · 178 Campbell Parade, Bondi Beach · 9130 3271 · Daily · 380, 382

ROYAL RANDWICK RACECOURSE

www.australianturfclub.com.au

This famous eastern suburbs racecourse with its six-level grandstand offers more than 50 horse-racing meetings each year.

B10 · Alison Road, Randwick · 9663 8400 · 372, 373, 374, 377

SEYMOUR THEATRE CENTRE

www.seymourcentre.com.au

In the heart of Sydney University campus and home to three diverse arts companies, this performing arts center has four performance venues plus foyers, a spacious courtyard and restaurant and bar facilities.

Off map · Corner of Cleveland Street and City Road, Chippendale · 9351 7940 for performance information · Redfern · 352, 370, 422, 428

SHARK DIVE XTREME

www.manlysealifesanctuary.com.au

View gray nurse sharks, stingrays and sea turtles up close in an aquarium environment.

Off map · West Esplanade, Manly · 8251 7878 · Daily · Manly

WHITEWATER RAFTING

www.penrithwhitewater.com.au

On the site of the Olympic kayaking events, this rafting and kayaking venue offers whitewater fun and thrills. Reservations essential.

Off map · McCarthy's Lane, Cranebrook · 4730 4333 · Daily 9–5 · Penrith Station

WATER SPORTS

Sydney's location offers unlimited opportunities for water sports. You can windsurf from Rose Bay (9371 7036), go diving at Coogee (9665 6333) or sail with the Northside Sailing School (9969 3972). Weekend surf carnivals, where lifesavers from opposing clubs compete, are held at beaches such as Bondi and Manly from October to March and you can watch competitive sailing on the water. The most exciting races, between 6m (19ft) long skiffs, are held on Saturday afternoons from mid-September to April—full details are available from the Sydney Flying Squadron (9955 8350).

Restaurants

Prices are approximate, based on a 3-course meal for one person.

$$$ over A$60
$$ A$40–A$60
$ under A$40

ASHCROFTS ($$$)

www.ashcrofts.com

One of the finest dining experiences in the upper Blue Mountains. Try the seared northern saucer scallops with Vietnamese mint and pickled ginger, or the slow-roast, corn-fed duck with spiced rum plums.

Off map 18 Govetts Leap Road, Blackheath 4787 8297 Thu–Sun dinner, Sun lunch

BONDI TRATTORIA ($$)

www.bonditrattoria.com.au

A café-cum-restaurant, which provides tempting Italian food and not-to-be-missed views over Bondi Beach.

Off map 34 Campbell Parade, Bondi Beach 9365 4303 Daily 7am–midnight 333, 380, 382

CATALINA ($$$)

www.catalinarosebay.com.au

One of Sydney's best; diners come here to be seen and to enjoy exquisite seafood on the classic, Mediterranean-inspired menu. Sushi and sashimi are a specialty (Wed–Sun).

Off map Lyne Park, Rose Bay 9371 0555 Mon–Sat 12–12, Sun 12–6 324, 325

DOYLES ON THE BEACH ($$$)

www.doyles.com.au

Sydney's most famous seafood restaurant, opened in 1885 and still in the same family, has great food and wonderful harbor views.

Off map 11 Marine Parade, Watsons Bay 9337 2007 Daily lunch, dinner 324, 325 Watsons Bay

DUNBAR HOUSE ($$$)

www.dunbarhouse.com.au

Lovely restored colonial house with beach and Sydney skyline views from the terrace. Its chic daytime café serves elegant offerings al fresco.

Off map 9 Marine Parade, Watsons Bay 9337 1226 Daily breakfast, lunch 324, 325 Watsons Bay

AUSTRALIAN WINES

Australian wines have taken the world by storm and are, for many, an integral part of dining out. There have been vineyards in New South Wales and other regions of the country since the 1820s. Most of these produce fine varieties such as Cabernet Sauvignon, Shiraz, Chardonnay and Chablis. There are hundreds of labels, but a few good wine-makers to look out for include Lindemans, Rosemount Estate, Houghtons, Wyndham Estate, Henschke, Tyrrell's, Penfolds and Wolf Blass.

ICEBERGS DINING ROOM ($$$)

www.idrb.com

Icebergs is elegant and fashionable, with the dining room, bar and terrace enjoying Bondi sea views. The food is regional Italian and the menu is seasonal.

Off map 1 Notts Avenue, Bondi Beach 9365 9000 Tue–Sun lunch, dinner 380, 382

RIVERBEND RESTAURANT ($$$)

A different, but limited, menu each evening featuring Modern Australian cuisine using fresh seasonal ingredients. Interesting wine list of mostly Australian wines.

Off map Old Northern Road, Wisemans Ferry 4560 0593 Daily 7am–10.30pm

SEAN'S PANAROMA ($$$)

Expect fresh seasonal produce transformed into innovative Med/Oz cuisine. The lovely sea views, attentive staff and good wine list are a bonus.

Off map 270 Campbell Parade, Bondi 9365 4924 Fri–Sun lunch, Wed–Sat dinner 380, 382

Sydney, with its high level of holiday visitors and businesspeople, offers every category of accommodations—from good-value budget options to international standard deluxe hotels.

Introduction

Sydney's diverse accommodations industry caters to all budgets. At the upper end there's the luxurious Park Hyatt Sydney, set right on the water's edge, and the Westin Sydney, occupying the classic old post office building in Martin Place. At the more lower-priced end, the ever popular Y on The Park offers good budget rooms with an excellent near-city location.

More Budget Choices

There are also many economical, self-catering apartments, and reasonably priced guesthouses and hostels are plentiful. Bed-and-breakfasts are numerous, especially in the outer suburbs and rural areas close to the city.

Where to Stay

Sydney's major hotel areas can be found downtown, around Darling Harbour and Pyrmont, Circular Quay, Central Railway and the inner eastern suburbs.

Get a Deal

It's worth looking on the internet for special deals, both in advance bookings and last-minute rate reductions. You can use the sites that compare and present hotels together, but if you have a good idea of the place you wish to stay, go directly to their website and look for a "specials" button. You can often get better deals this way. But be aware that there are popular times of the year, such as around New Year and January, when hotels are fully booked, so forward booking at this time of year is essential.

STAY AT THE AIRPORT

Although Sydney's CBD is only 11km (7 miles) from the international airport, there are times when a stay at an airport hotel is necessary. Fortunately there are some good options: Ibis Budget Sydney Airport (☎ 8339 1840) is nearer the Domestic terminal; Rydges Sydney Airport (☎ 9313 2500) is within the International terminal, and Airport Sydney International Inn (☎ 9556 1555) in the quieter suburb of Arncliffe, offers a shuttle bus service.

From modern boutique hotels to Victorian guest-houses—it's all here in Sydney

Budget Hotels

PRICES

Expect to pay under A$150 for a double room per night in a budget hotel.

AARONS HOTEL SYDNEY

www.aaronsydney. com.au

Better-than-average accommodations, near to Darling Harbour, with 24-hour reception services. It has 93 rooms, as well as a restaurant and bar.

C8 37 Ultimo Road, Haymarket 1800 101 100 Central

AUSTRALIAN SUNRISE LODGE

www.australiansunriselodge.com

Good choice of single or double rooms, most with private balcony and bathrooms. Well located in the vibrant suburb of Newtown, with a total of 22 rooms.

Off map 485 King Street, Newtown 9550 4999 422 Newtown

BLUE MOUNTAINS YHA

www.yha.com.au

This pleasant hostel includes a lounge area and games room. Large dorm rooms sleep eight people, but there are double and twin rooms, many with ensuites. Plenty of breathtaking views close by, plus pubs and restaurants.

Off map 207 Katoomba Street, Katoomba 4782 1416 Katoomba

BONDI BEACHOUSE YHA

www.yha.com.au

A 20-minute bus ride to either the airport or CBD, this popular 50-room hostel includes double rooms with private bath. Stay by the beach, yet close to all the action in the city—perfect.

Off map 63 Fletcher Street, Bondi Beach 9365 2088 380, 381, 382

CREMORNE POINT MANOR

www.cremornepointmanor.com.au

On the north shore, this spacious 30-room manor house provides kitchens, laundry service, free WiFi and a continental breakfast.

G3 6 Cremorne Road, Cremorne Point 9953 7899 Cremorne Point

BUDGET STAYS

In addition to many budget hotels, Sydney has dozens of good, inexpensive backpackers' lodges. Prices start at A$20 per night and many establishments offer reduced rates for long stays. Accommodations vary from private rooms to dormitories and the best backpacker areas are Kings Cross, inner-west Glebe and beach suburbs such as Bondi and Coogee. Another budget option is staying in a "hotel". In Australia, the word hotel has two definitions: it can mean either a conventional hotel or a pub with rooms.

IBIS BUDGET SYDNEY EAST

www.accorhotels.com

Economy hotel with 115 rooms close to transport and the lively Kings Cross nightlife.

F8 191–201 William Street, Kings Cross 9326 0300 Kings Cross

NOAH'S ON BONDI

www.noahsbondibeach.com

Popular budget choice with shared facilities. Billiard table, internet and TV room.

Off map 2 Campbell Parade, Bondi Beach 9365 7100 380, 382, 389

SYDNEY CENTRAL YHA

www.yha.com

In a heritage-listed building near Central Station, it's excellent for backpackers. You don't need a hostel card to stay in one of the 140 rooms.

D8 Corner of Pitt Street and Rawson Place 9218 9099 Central Kings Cross

Y ON THE PARK

www.yhotel.com.au

On the edge of the CBD, this spotless and popular hotel has 127 rooms.

D8 5–11 Wentworth Avenue 9264 2451 Museum

Mid-Range Hotels

PRICES

Expect to pay between A$150 and A$300 per night for a double room in a mid-range hotel.

1888 HOTEL

www.1888hotel.com.au

A boutique hotel in a restored wool store with exposed brick walls, original beams and luxury bathrooms with walk-in rain showers. There's an Eatery and Bar and guests get free passes to the nearby Ian Thorpe Aquatic Centre.

B7 · 139 Murray Street, Pyrmont · 8586 1888 · Light Rail to Pyrmont · Darling Harbour

CAMBRIDGE

www.cambridgehotel.com.au

A friendly, 149-room hotel close to Oxford Street, within walking distance of the CBD and with good transport links. There's a spa and a heated pool. The rustic Italian restaurant serves breakfast and dinner every day. Book direct on the website and receive free WiFi.

E8 · 121 Riley Street, Surry HIlls · 9212 1111 · Central · 370, 380

THE CARRINGTON HOTEL

www.thecarrington.com.au

Named in 1886 after Lord Carrington, a former Governor of New South Wales at that time, this grand hotel is, in the Blue Mountains and is National Trust listed. It offers all mod cons, fine dining, a grand high tea every Sunday and a spa.

Off map · 15–47 Katoomba Street, Katoomba · 4782 111 · Katoomba

HARBOUR ROCKS HOTEL

www.mgallery.com

Cleverly restored historic building at the heart of The Rocks, a great location for exploring top Sydney sights. The 59 rooms are decorated in heritage colors, there's a good restaurant, friendly bar and small fitness center.

D4 · 34 Harrington Street, The Rocks · 8220 9999 · Circular Quay

THE HUGHENDEN BOUTIQUE HOTEL

www.thehughenden.com.au

Located in the heart of Paddington, this Victorian manor boutique hotel offers 36 rooms.

H10 · 14 Queen Street, Woollahra · 9363 4863 · 378, 380

APARTMENTS

Apartment-style hotels in Sydney generally fall into the mid-range price category. These so-called serviced apartments vary from one to three bedrooms, with separate dining areas and kitchens or kitchenettes, and most larger apartments have private laundry facilities. Many are large enough for families or small groups.

IBIS DARLING HARBOUR

www.accorhotels.com.au

This is a modern hotel close to many of Sydney's major attractions. All rooms have all the usual facilities, plus broadband high-speed internet access and LCD TV. The hotel restaurant serves breakfast and dinner.

B7 · 70 Murray Street, Pyrmont · 9563 0888 · Central

KIRKETON BOUTIQUE HOTEL

www.8hotels.com

This boutique designer hotel is stylish and hip and has 40 rooms. There is a good Asian restaurant.

F8 · 229 Darlinghurst Road, Darlinghurst · 9332 2011 · Kings Cross

THE MACLEAY APARTMENT HOTEL

www.themacleay.com

Comfortable rooms with all facilities and services, as well as studio apartments with kitchenettes and private bathrooms. Many rooms have city and Harbour views.

F7 · 28 Macleay Street, Potts Point · 9357 7755 · Kings Cross

METRO APARTMENTS ON DARLING HARBOUR

www.metrohotels.com.au

Enjoy the excellent view of Darling Harbour from

these apartments, which are in two adjacent buildings on the west side of the city. They include fully serviced one-bedroom suites and apartments. King Street has 10 apartments, rooftop pool and barbecue facilities; Sussex Street has 30 apartments. All sleep up to four people and have a balcony, fully equipped kitchen, living and dining area, shower and bath.

C7 ✉ 132–136 Sussex Street ☎ 9199 2517 Town Hall

MORGANS OF SYDNEY

www.morganshotel.com.au

Choose from 26 spacious and elegantly furnished suites, all with queen-size beds. Rooftop deck.

F8 ✉ 304 Victoria Street, Darlinghurst ☎ 8354 3444 Kings Cross

PEPPERS GUEST HOUSE

www.peppers.com.au/guest-house

This upscale guesthouse is surrounded by lush, beautiful gardens, and also boasts a fine dining restaurant, Chez Pok. The colonial-style rooms in the traditional building have all modern amenities, as do the four rooms in the separate, self-contained homestead. Check the website for last-minute deals.

Off map ✉ Ekerts Road, Pokolbin, Hunter Valley ☎ 4993 8999

QUALITY HOTEL CKS SYDNEY AIRPORT

www.airportinn.com.au

Close to the Domestic and International terminals and with a shuttle bus service, this property provides comfortable, convenient accommodations, a restaurant and an internet kiosk.

Off map ✉ 35 Levey Street, Arncliffe ☎ 9556 1555 Wolli Creek

RAVESI'S ON BONDI BEACH

www.ravesis.com.au

A boutique hotel with 12 tastefully decorated and furnished rooms and suites, with views overlooking Bondi Beach. There is a restaurant and cocktail bar.

Off map ✉ 118 Campbell Parade, Bondi Beach ☎ 9365 4422 380, 382

THE RUSSELL

www.therussell.com.au

This delightful Victorian building has been renovated to provide boutique-style accommodations. The sitting room and its bar, furnished in period style, open on to a balcony over George Street. There is a rooftop garden and the bedrooms are all furnished in Victorian style. Breakfast is served downstairs in the Fortune of War, Sydney's oldest pub.

D4 ✉ 143A George Street, The Rocks ☎ 9241 3543 Circular Quay

LOCATION

As with all large cities, you may need to make a compromise on your hotel location in Sydney. While CBD hotels are close to rail and bus services, those around Circular Quay and The Rocks also enjoy proximity to ferry services. Accommodations in the eastern suburbs have rail and bus connections and are often set in pleasant, quiet locations.

VICTORIA COURT HOTEL SYDNEY

www.victoriacourt.com.au

This charming 1881-built Victorian bed and breakfast hotel has a wonderfully verdant courtyard conservatory. These very comfortable accommodations make for an enjoyable stay. There are 25 rooms.

F7 ✉ 122 Victoria Street, Potts Point ☎ 9357 3200 Kings Cross

THE YORK BY SWISS-BELHOTEL

www.theyorkapartments.com.au

These 120 suites and residences are close to Darling Harbour and the CBD. Suites range in size from studio to two-bedroomed executive apartments, all have a full kitchen, bathroom, laundry and balcony. The apartments are serviced daily.

D6 ✉ 5 York Street ☎ 9210 5000 Wynyard

Luxury Hotels

PRICES

Expect to pay over A$300 per night for a double room at a luxury hotel.

FOUR POINTS BY SHERATON

www.starwoodhotels.com

A glossy, deluxe hotel with 683 rooms, overlooking Darling Harbour. Australia's biggest hotel, it blends modern design with its historic buildings, including the 1850s Dundee Arms Pub.

C7 161 Sussex Street 9290 4000 Town Hall Sydney Aquarium

FOUR SEASONS HOTEL

www.fourseasons.com

The Four Seasons, with 531 rooms and overlooking Sydney Harbour, has a pampering spa, pool and fitness center. The hotel's Woods restaurant offers fine dining around a wood-fired oven and open kitchen.

D5 199 George Street 9250 3100 Circular Quay

HOTEL INTERCONTINENTAL SYDNEY

www.intercontinental.com

Close to the Botanic Gardens and The Rocks, this 503-room hotel is based on the historic 1851 Treasury Building. The Café Opera offers French-inspired fine dining, or choose from the superb buffet with its theatrical dessert displays. Dine alfresco amid the hotel's historic sandstone arcades.

D5 117 Macquarie Street 9253 9000 1240 Circular Quay

LILIANFELS BLUE MOUNTAINS HOTEL

www.lilianfels.com.au

This luxurious hotel, which includes a gym, spa and infinity pool, has rooms that are individually decorated, each with an opulent bathroom. The renowned and elegant Darley's restaurant serves Modern Australian cuisine.

Off map Lilianfels Avenue, Echo Point, Katoomba 4780 1200 Katoomba

PARK HYATT SYDNEY

www.sydney.park.hyatt.com

In terms of waterside location, this hotel with 158 rooms including suites has it all, plus direct views of the Harbour Bridge and Opera House. Elegant restaurant.

D4 7 Hickson Road, The Rocks 9256 1234 Circular Quay

INTERNET SPECIALS

It is often possible to secure luxury accommodations for the price of a lesser quality property by searching the internet for seasonal and last-minute special deals. Besides the individual hotel websites, always worth going to first, general hotel comparison sites allow you to compare deals for a variety of hotels, book online, and even earn future credits on the transaction.

SHANGRI-LA HOTEL SYDNEY

www.shangri-la.com

This hotel offers wonderful views over the Harbour. There are 10 dining and other entertainment facilities and the cocktail bar has superb panoramic views for just the price of a drink. There are 561 rooms.

D5 176 Cumberland Street, The Rocks 9250 6000 Circular Quay

SHERATON ON THE PARK

www.sheratontheparksydney.com

This magnificent central hotel has a grand three-floor lobby, a rooftop health club and a fine restaurant. Excellent views. 557 rooms.

D7 161 Elizabeth Street 9286 6000 St. James

WESTIN SYDNEY

www.westinsydney.com

Part of the old Sydney GPO, this international hotel has 416 rooms, ultra-lavish facilities and features a heritage section with rooms furnished in period style.

D6 1 Martin Place 8223 1111 Circular Quay

Need to Know

Sydney is the tourist capital of Australia, and the more you plan your trip, the more you'll get out of it. Use these pages to familiarize yourself with travel options and gain useful insider knowledge of the city.

Planning Ahead

When to Go

Sydney's tourist months are December to February. March and April or September and October are better times to visit, as the crowds have thinned and the weather is warm and sunny. It is advisable to take an umbrella as subtropical thunderstorms are common.

TIME

Sydney is 9 hours ahead of the UK, 14 hours ahead of New York and 17 hours ahead of Los Angeles.

AVERAGE DAILY MAXIMUM TEMPERATURES

JAN	FEB	MAR	APR	MAY	JUN	JUL	AUG	SEP	OCT	NOV	DEC
79°F	79°F	77°F	72°F	66°F	63°F	61°F	64°F	68°F	72°F	75°F	77°F
26°C	26°C	25°C	22°C	19°C	17°C	16°C	18°C	20°C	22°C	24°C	25°C

Spring (September to November) is warm with sunny days that are mostly dry; the nights are cool to mild.

Summer (December to February) is warm to very hot but can also be humid and rather wet. Thunderstorms are common.

Fall (March to May) sees mild to warm days with mild to cool nights. This season is generally dry.

Winter (June to August) is mostly dry with mild, sunny days and cool nights. Take a medium-weight coat.

WHAT'S ON

January *Sydney Festival:* A three-week long cultural celebration.
International cricket matches: Sydney Cricket Ground.
Australia Day (26 Jan): The nation celebrates its birthday with fireworks.
February *Chinese New Year:* Fireworks and feasting in Chinatown.
February/March *Gay and Lesbian Mardi Gras:* The city's biggest street parade.
March/April *The Golden Slipper:* A horse race.
Anzac Day (25 Apr): War Veterans Parade.
Royal Easter Show: Agriculture show, Sydney Showground.
May *Sydney Writers' Festival:* National and international speakers.
June *Sydney Film Festival:* Films from many nations.
August *City-to-Surf:* A 14-km (9-mile) run to Bondi Beach.
September/October *Rugby Grand Finals:* League and union teams battle it out in their respective finals.
October *Manly Jazz Festival:* Music by the sea.
November *Neighbourhood Festivals:* Double Bay and Newtown, stalls, music.
December *Sydney to Hobart Race* (26 Dec): Start of one of the world's great yacht races.
Tropfest: Outdoor short-film festival.

Listings Check the *Sydney Morning Herald.* On Fridays this newspaper publishes a 20-page guide, detailing everything from opera to free outdoor events. Other publications are *This Week in Sydney* and *What's On in Sydney*, available from hotels and tourist kiosks.

Sydney Online

At the heart of Australia's digital culture, Sydney has excellent websites with regular information on everything from the cinema to local news, weather and listings of hotels and restaurants.

www.sydney.com
The official Sydney website. A complete guide with travel information, and listings of hotels and events in the city.

www.sydneyoperahouse.com
Look here for listings of performances and events at the Sydney Opera House—a must-see for everyone—with a booking option and a virtual tour.

www.discoversydney.com.au
General information for Sydney. Includes what to see and do, where to eat, shop and stay.

www.sydneyairport.com.au
Flight information and all you need to know at the airport including hotels and shopping.

www.smh.com.au
The *Sydney Morning Herald's* website gives up-to-date information on dining, nightlife and events news.

www.sydneyaccommodationonline.com
A guide to hotels, shopping, attractions and restaurants.

www.visitnsw.com
What to see and do in New South Wales, destinations, visitor information centers and accommodations.

www.au.timeout.com/sydney
The go-to site for food and drink reviews and what's on day and night in Sydney.

GOOD TRAVEL SITES

www.fodors.com
A travel-planning site where you can research prices and weather; book tickets, cars and rooms; and link to other sites.

www.transportnsw.info
Information about timetables, routes and fares for buses, trains and ferries.

www.cityofsydney.nsw.gov.au
Practical tips on the city and what's on information.

CYBERCAFÉS

Central Internet Café
Includes copying, faxing and CD-burning facilities.
D8 Shop 1/230 Elizabeth Street 9281 9988 Daily 9am–2am A$5 per half hour

Global Gossip
Internet, inexpensive phone calls; discounts for all Global Gossip outlets.
F7 111 Darlinghurst Road, Kings Cross 9326 9777 Daily 9am–midnight A$5 per half hour

City Hunter CyberCafé
Largest gaming-oriented internet café chain.
C8 374 Sussex Street, Chinatown 9261 0768 Daily 8am–midnight A$5 per half hour

Getting There

ENTRY REQUIREMENTS

All visitors to Australia require a valid passport and an Electronic Travel Authority (ETA), which has replaced the traditional visa.
A Tourist ETA is valid for multiple travel within one year (or the expiry date of your passport, if sooner) on three-month visits. An ETA is available through most travel agents, as well as overseas Australian diplomatic offices. Australia does not allow entry if your passport expires within six months of your entry date.

BEFORE YOU GO

- Vaccination certificates are not normally required, unless you have visited an infected country within the previous 14 days.
- Tourism Australia: Mailbox 358, 2029 Century Park E Ste. 3150, Los Angeles, CA 90067 ☎ 310 695 3200

AIRPORT

Sydney International Airport is the main port of entry for travelers arriving by air. There are numerous daily flights, buses and train services to Sydney from all major towns and cities in Australia.

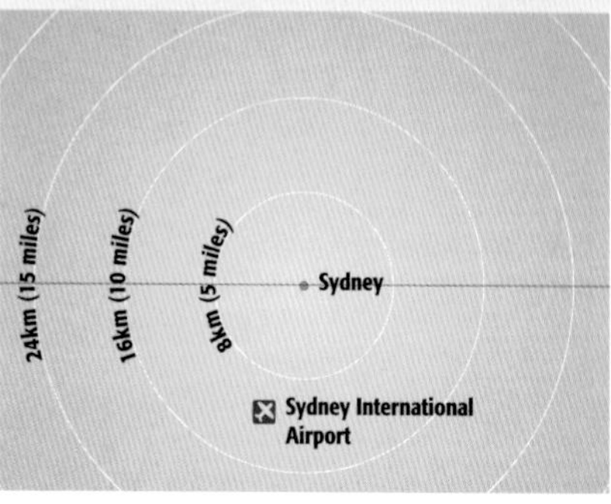

ARRIVING BY AIR

Sydney Airport (☎ 9967 9111; www.sydneyairport.com.au) at Mascot, south of the city, is the main port of entry for overseas visitors on direct flights. The airport also handles the majority of domestic passenger arrivals. The airport is a short distance from Sydney's CBD. There are taxis, a rail service and bus services, as well as car rental outlets. This includes the KST Sydney Airporter (☎ 9666 9988), which travels into the city every 20–30 minutes for A$15, going to all accommodations and hostels, in the Kings Cross, city and Darling Harbour areas.

Sydney trains take 15 minutes from the airport to central Sydney, and the cost is A$17.20 for a one-way trip.

A taxi from the airport into the city takes 20–40 minutes (depending on traffic) and costs around A$50.

ARRIVING BY BUS

Bus travel is often more expensive than flying, but buses are nevertheless one of the best ways to see more of Australia on your

way to Sydney. Country and interstate buses pick up and depart from the Transit Centre at the Eddy Avenue side of Central Station. Daylight and overnight buses arrive each day from Melbourne and Brisbane and usually take between 8 and 12 hours respectively. The main interstate carrier is Greyhound Australia (☎ 1300 473 946; www.greyhound.com.au).

ARRIVING BY CAR

Car rental is inexpensive in Australia and is a popular way for families to save money on inter-capital travel. The main highways between cities are excellent. Sydney and larger regional hubs have several car rental firms, offering a variety of vehicles and deals. You must be at least 25 years old, and you can pay additional fees to have the insurance excess waived. The main rental companies are Avis, Budget, Europcar, Hertz, National and Thrifty.

ARRIVING BY SEA

Not the most common means by which to arrive in Sydney, although the city is a very popular port for cruise liners. Celebrity Cruises, Holland America, Royal Caribbean, Princess Cruises and many more include Sydney on their cruise schedules. Sydney's Overseas Passenger Terminal, at Circular Quay, services cruise ships.

ARRIVING BY TRAIN

Regional and Intercity trains (☎ 132 232; www.nswtrainlink.info) travel to and around New South Wales and offer a comfortable way to see the state and the country. The Trainlink trains arrive at Central Station, part of the metropolitan train system's underground City Loop service. The XPT train service from Melbourne to Sydney takes around 10–11 hours. The Indian Pacific, running from Sydney to Perth via Adelaide, connects two oceans in one of the world's longest train journeys. Enjoy the sights from your cabin, and take a range of optional off-train sightseeing tours along the way.

INSURANCE

Check your policy and buy any necessary supplements. It is vital that travel insurance covers medical expenses, in addition to accident, trip cancellation, baggage loss and theft. Check the policy covers any continuing treatment for a chronic condition.

VISITORS WITH DISABILITIES

Most of Sydney's attractions are suitable for visitors using a wheelchair, with ramped public buildings and accessible buses, ferries, rail stations and taxis. Some hotels have roll-in showers, and some have Braille signage. For details, check out www.sydneyforall.com.au and easyaccessaustralia.com.au/sydney.

Older buildings are often retrofitted with ramped access and many National Trust properties are at least partially accessible. Many Sydney attractions have hearing loops. You'll usually find parking places for drivers with disabilities, although you'll need a temporary permit from the Roads and Traffic Authority to use them (☎ 13 2213).

TAXI

Getting Around

DRIVING

- Driving is on the left and overtaking traffic (which has the right of way) is on the right. This, however, may not be immediately obvious on multilane highways, where the preference seems to be to stay in the right-hand lane. On some stretches of winding roads, lay-bys are provided to be used by slow traffic to enable other drivers to overtake.
- Take special care when driving on unsurfaced roads; they are best avoided. Also, avoid driving in the country at night; and beware of stray animals on motorways at dawn and dusk.
- Some road signs are peculiar to Australia, but most will be immediately understandable to visitors.
- Full details of Australia's road rules are available at www.aaa.asn.au.
- Speed limits are 50/60kph (31/37mph) in urban areas and 100/110kph (62/68mph) elsewhere unless indicated.
- Seatbelts must be worn in front and back seats.
- Fuel (unleaded and super unleaded) is sold by the liter; gas stations are numerous but may have restricted weekend opening hours.
- The legal limit for alcohol is 0.05 percent blood alcohol level.

Sydney is compact and much of it can be explored on foot, but taxis are plentiful. The city has a good transit system of buses and ferries, as well as a partly underground city and suburban rail system (☎ 131 500). Free public transport maps are available from bus, ferry and train offices at Circular Quay, Wynyard bus station and Town Hall train station.

The efficient Airport Rail Link (www.airportlink.com.au) runs from the International and Domestic terminals at Sydney Airport to the City Circle train line, stopping at Central, Museum, St. James, Circular Quay, Wynyard and Town Hall stations. Trains run about every 10 minutes and the complete trip takes around 20 minutes.

BY BUS

Sydney's buses are blue and white. The most important bus stations are Circular Quay (to Bondi Beach, the eastern suburbs, the south and some inner-west areas) and Wynyard (over Harbour Bridge). A smart card system operates across Sydney's entire public transport network—the Opal Card. When boarding a bus, train or ferry you need to tap the card against an Opal card reader and tap again (and listen for the 'ding' tone that indicates it has registered) when leaving at the end of your journey. The display screen shows the fare deducted and any value left on the card. The daily travel cost is capped at A$15 (adults, A$7.50 child/youth), A$2.50 on Sundays.

Free Sydney shuttle buses operate in a loop around the CBD. The green buses run every 10 minutes between Central Station and Circular Quay via George Street on weekdays from 9–3.30 (Thu 9pm) and Sat–Sun 9-6. The route number for the free CBD shuttle is 555, you board at stops displaying the green shuttle logo and do not need a ticket to travel. The buses are wheelchair accessible.

Sydney and Bondi Explorer (www.theaustralianexplorer.com.au) are red, hop on-hop off, open-top city and beach tour buses. A one-day ticket costs A$40 (adult), family pass A$110.

BY BOAT

Ferry services operate from four wharves on Circular Quay to 30 places around Sydney Harbour, including Manly and Taronga Zoo, and up-river to Homebush Bay and Parramatta. Buy tickets from the Circular Quay counters, Wharf 4 or use an Opal card. Water taxis operate along the Harbour; Yellow Water Taxis are the main operator ☎ 9299 0199.

BY CAR

You must be over 25 to rent a car and have a home country or international driver's license. Compulsory third-party insurance is included in rental prices, which are on average A$70–A$100 per day. Major Sydney car-rental companies include: Avis ☎ 136 333; Budget ☎ 1300 362 848; Hertz ☎ 133 039.

BY TAXI

Cabs are abundant and fares are reasonable by world standards. Main operators include: Legion Cabs ☎ 131451; Taxis Combined Services ☎ 133 300; Premier Cabs ☎ 131017; Yellow Cabs ☎ 136 294; Zero200, wheelchair accessible taxis ☎ 8332 0200.

BY TRAIN

A light rail service connects Central Station to Chinatown, Darling Harbour, Star City casino and the Sydney Fish Market. Sydney's inner-city rail services include the City Circle (Central, Town Hall, Wynyard, Circular Quay, St. James and Museum) and the Eastern Suburbs Line, which runs from Central to Town Hall, Martin Place, Kings Cross, Edgecliff and Bondi Junction. Off-peak tickets (weekends and weekdays after 9am) represent a 45 percent saving.

FURTHER INFORMATION

- For timetable and transportation ticket information ☎ 131 500 🕐 Daily 6am–10pm
- Trainlink train information ☎ 132 232
- Useful websites: www.opal.com.au; www.sydneybuses.info; www.sydneytrains.info.

TOURIST INFORMATION

- Sydney Information Line ☎ 9911 7700
- Sydney Visitor Centre at The Rocks; www.sydney.com ✉ Level 1, The Rocks Centre, corner Argyle and Playfair Streets ☎ 8273 0000 🕐 Daily 9.30–5.30. Closed Good Fri, 25 Dec. Information, accommodations bookings
- Sydney Visitor Centre Darling Harbour ✉ 33 Wheat Road, Darling Harbour ☎ 9211 4288 🕐 Daily 9.30–5.30. Closed Good Fri, 25 Dec
- Tourism New South Wales ☎ 9240 8788; www.visitnsw.com
- Tourism Australia (www.tourism.australia.com) offices outside Australia: USA ✉ Mailbox 358, 2029 Century Park E Ste. 3150, Los Angeles, CA 90067 ☎ 310 695 3200; UK ✉ 6th floor, Australia House, Melbourne Place, Strand, London WC2B 4LG ☎ 020 7438 4600

ETIQUETTE

Smoking is prohibited on public transport (including inside airport terminals), in restaurants, cinemas, halls and shops and shopping malls. Tipping (normally 10 percent) is expected only in restaurants where service charges are not added to bills. Tipping taxi-drivers and hotel staff is optional.

TAXI

Essential Facts

PLACES OF WORSHIP

- Roman Catholic: St. Mary's Cathedral ✉ St. Mary's Road
- Presbyterian: Scots Church ✉ 44 Margaret Street
- Baptist Church: Central Baptist ✉ 619 George Street
- Interdenominational: Wayside Chapel ✉ 29 Hughes Street, Kings Cross
- Jewish: The Great Synagogue ✉ 166 Castlereagh Street
- Buddhist: Buddhist Centre ☎ 9519 0440
- Muslim: Erskineville Mosque ✉ 13 John Street

MONEY

The Australian unit of currency is the Australian dollar (A$), comprising 100 cents (¢). Banknotes come in denominations of 100, 50, 20, 10 and 5 dollars. Coins come in 5, 10, 20 and 50 cents (silver), and 1 and 2 dollars (gold-colored).

ELECTRICITY

The electricity supply in Australia is 230–250 volts AC. Three-flat-pin plugs are the standard (although note that they are unlike British plugs). Hotels provide standard 110-volt and 240-volt shaver sockets.

EMERGENCY PHONE NUMBERS

- Police, ambulance or fire ☎ 000 (24 hours). All calls for these services are free.
- Dental, pharmaceutical, personal, or other: See the front of the A–K volume of the Sydney White Pages telephone book (www.whitepages.com.au) or www.sydney.com.au/emergen.htm.

MEDICAL TREATMENT

- Medical, dental and ambulance services are excellent but costly.
- Doctors and dentists are readily available and there are many medical facilities where appointments are not necessary.
- Hotel Doctor Service ☎ 9962 6000 🕐 Daily 24 hours (applies only to Central Sydney hotels).

MEDICINES

You may bring in prescribed medications. Keep them in the original containers and bring a copy of your doctor's prescription to avoid problems at customs.

NEWSPAPERS AND MAGAZINES

- The main national newspaper is *The Australian.*
- The major city newspaper is the *Sydney Morning Herald.*
- For business, financial and investment news see *The Australian Financial Review.*

OPENING HOURS

- Shops: generally Mon–Fri 9–5.30, Sat 9–4. Late-night shopping until 9 on Thu. Large stores open Sun until 4. Suburban corner shops often open daily 8–8 or later.
- Post offices: Mon–Fri 9–5. Sydney GPO hours are Mon–Fri 8.15–5.30, Sat 8.30–2.

• Banks: Mon–Thu 9.30–4, Fri 9.30–5. City head-office banks open Mon–Fri 8.15–5.

POSTAL SERVICES

• Larger post offices provide services such as passport and ID photos, money transfers and foreign currency.
• Stamps can also be purchased from hotels, and from some newsstands and souvenir shops.
• Postage information ☎ 131318.

PUBLIC HOLIDAYS

1 Jan, 26 Jan (Australia Day), Good Fri, Easter Mon, 25 Apr (Anzac Day), 2nd Mon in Jun (Queen's birthday), 1st Mon in Aug (NSW; banks only), 1st Mon in Oct (Labour Day: NSW state holiday), 25–26 Dec. School summer holidays are mid-December to late January. As a result transport and tourist facilities are very busy and accommodation is heavily reserved at this time.

SENSIBLE PRECAUTIONS

• Report theft or any other incident to your hotel and/or the police as soon as possible. If your traveler's checks are stolen, advise the relevant organization.
• The non-emergency police inquiries number is ☎ 9281 0000.
• Sydney's police wear blue uniforms and a peaked cap or baseball cap. They are generally helpful and polite.
• Tap water is safe to drink; the only medical problems you are likely to experience are sunburn and mosquito bites.
• If you burn easily, generously apply at least sunblock SPF15+, wear sunglasses, a broad-brimmed hat and long sleeves, and avoid the summer sun from 11 to 3.
• Dangerous currents and marine stingers can cause problems in the sea in summer, so take notice of lifeguards and any beach signs.
• Women are generally safe in Sydney, but walking alone in parks or on beaches at night and traveling alone on trains out of the central city area is not recommended.

CUSTOMS REGULATIONS

• Visitors aged 18 or over may bring in 50 cigarettes or 50g of tobacco or cigars; 2.25 liters of alcohol; plus other dutiable goods to the value of A$900 per person.
• There is no limit on money imported for personal use, although amounts in excess of A$10,000 or its equivalent must be declared on arrival.
• Animals are subject to quarantine, and goods of plant or animal origin must be declared on arrival. It is forbidden to bring in food.
• Drugs smuggling is treated very seriously and harshly, and importing firearms and products from endangered species is illegal or restricted.

STUDENTS

Australia is a preferred destination for students, either enjoying a vacation or taking a gap year from their studies. The country has an extensive array of inexpensive hostel and backpacker accommodations, and travel options include bus, rail and air services that are not too expensive if booked well in advance. Students can supplement their income by a range of part-time work. Be sure to apply online for a Working Holiday visa (www.immi.gov.au) before you enter the country.

CASH AND CREDIT CARDS

Currency exchanges at hotels, some shops, tourist areas and outlets such as American Express and Thomas Cook are open outside banking hours. Airport exchange facilities are open daily 5.30am–11pm. You can obtain cash from 24-hour cash machines (ATMs) throughout the city and country. Major credit cards (American Express, Visa and MasterCard) are widely accepted. A 10 percent goods and services tax is automatically added to your purchases however, if you buy goods valued at A$300 or more from any one supplier you can claim the tax back from the designated booths at Sydney Airport.

CONSULATES

- Canada ☎ 9364 3000
- France ☎ 9261 5779
- Germany ☎ 9328 7733
- UK ☎ 9247 7521
- USA ☎ 9373 9200

TELEPHONES

- Public telephones are found at phone booths, post offices, hotels, service stations, shops, rail and bus stations and cafés. Local calls cost 50¢ for unlimited time (20¢ and 10¢ coins can be used).
- Long-distance calls within Australia, known as STD, vary in price, but you should have a good supply of 50¢ and A$1 coins. Calls are less expensive after 6pm and all day Sunday.
- Operator assistance and directory assistance: ☎ 1223 (Australia), 1225 (International).
- Reverse-charge (collect) calls: ☎ 12 550.
- Phonecards come in values of A$2 to A$20; credit cards can also be used from some (silver) phones. International Calling Cards, available at newsagents, can cut the cost of international calls.
- For international (IDD) calls (can be made from some public phones) dial 0011 followed by the country codes: US and Canada 1; UK 44; France 33; Germany 49.
- To call Australia from the US dial 011 61; from the UK dial 00 61, then drop the initial zero from the area code.
- To call a Sydney number from outside the metropolitan area, use the prefix 02.

TELEVISION AND RADIO

- ABC (Australian Broadcasting Corporation) and SBS (Special Broadcasting Service) have no commercials.
- Sydney has three commercial stations: Channels 7, 9 and 10.
- Cable and satellite services are available in most major hotels.
- Sydney has many commercial radio stations and a network of community radio stations. The ABC runs a national public radio network, which includes Classic FM and Radio National, a news and information station.

TOILETS

Free restrooms are found in parks, public places, galleries and museums, department stores and bus and train stations.

Language

Most people understand the greeting "G'day" as being Australian slang for "hello". But there are lots of other less familiar words and phrases that you're likely to encounter on a trip to Australia. Australians sometimes say several words as one "waddayareckon" ("what do you reckon?") and "owyagoin" ("how are you going?"). Listed here are the meanings of some of the words and phrases you'll most likely hear.

AUSSIE ENGLISH

ankle biter	*small or young child*
arvo	*afternoon*
barney	*argument, fight*
big smoke	*the city*
bloke	*man*
bonza	*excellent, attractive*
bush	*the country*
chinwag	*chat, conversation*
cobber	*mate, friend*
dag	*person with little dress sense, uncouth*
drongo	*slow-witted person*
dunny	*outside toilet*
fair dinkum	*genuine, true*
full as a boot	*intoxicated*
get stuffed	*go away*
hard yakka	*hard work*
hooroo	*goodbye*
knock off	*to steal something, a counterfeit product*
larrikin	*lout, mischievous*
pommie	*English person*
rack off	*go away, get lost*
sheila	*girl, woman*
skite	*boast, brag*
slab	*carton of 24 beer cans*
struth!	*exclamation of surprise*
stubby	*small bottle of beer*
sunnies	*pair of sunglasses*
tee up	*to organize something*
tinnie	*can of beer*
true blue	*genuine*
tucker	*food*
yarn	*story*
yonks	*long period of time*

Timeline

THE FIRST FLEET

The unusual birth of modern Australia might so easily have been a disastrous false start, but Sydney and the nation have thrived, thanks initially to Governor Phillip and the people who traveled on the First Fleet of 11 ships from England. These reluctant pioneers of 1788—including 568 male and 191 female convicts, and 200 marines and their wives and children—suffered incredible hardships to set this isolated colony on its feet. For the first two years, lack of farming skills meant near starvation, and it was only the fortuitous arrival of supply ships from England that saved the day.

40,000–50,000BC Aborigines arrive from Southeast Asia.

AD1770 Captain James Cook and the crew of the *Endeavour* arrive at Botany Bay.

1779 Suggestions are made in England that New South Wales could become a penal colony.

1787 The First Fleet sails from Portsmouth, England. The 11 ships carry more than 1,400 people.

1788 The First Fleet arrives at Botany Bay. The commander and first governor of the colony, Captain Arthur Phillip, deems the site unsuitable and moves his settlement north to Port Jackson (Sydney Harbour). The colony of New South Wales is proclaimed.

1793 The first free settlers land in Sydney.

1804 An uprising of 400 Irish convicts occurs at Castle Hill. Australia's second settlement is founded at Hobart, Tasmania.

1813 A route over the previously impenetrable Blue Mountains is finally discovered by explorers Wentworth, Lawson and Blaxland, opening up Australia's agricultural potential.

1832 Assisted passages over the next 140 years help millions of people, mainly Britons, to emigrate to Australia.

The Endeavour *sailing towards Tahiti in 1769, en route for Australia (left); panoramic view of Sydney Harbour (middle); International Aquatic Centre, home to the 2000 Olympic swimming competitions (right)*

1840 Convict transportation to New South Wales ends.

1851 Gold is discovered near Bathurst, and Sydney's population doubles in 10 years.

1900 Bubonic plague breaks out in The Rocks.

1901 The Commonwealth of Australia is proclaimed at Centennial Park on 1 January, joining the six Australian colonies into a federation.

1914–18 and 1939–45 Australian troops fight overseas during World War I and II.

1947 Post-war immigration from Europe begins, boosting skilled workers.

1992 The 150th anniversary of Sydney's city status.

1999 Australia votes against becoming a republic.

2000 Sydney hosts the Olympic Games.

2003 Australian troops join US forces in the war on Iraq.

2013 Severe bush fires wreak devastation in the Blue Mountains and across NSW.

2015 Australia hosts the soccer AFC Asian Cup—the first country outside of Asia to do so.

GOLD FEVER

Although declared a city in 1842, it was not until the 1851 discovery of gold near Bathurst, beyond the Blue Mountains, that Sydney really came of age. Word soon spread and prospectors arrived from all over the world. Sydney boomed, and its population virtually doubled in a decade.

Index

TITLES IN THE SERIES

- Amsterdam
- Barcelona
- Boston
- Budapest
- Chicago
- Dubai
- Dublin
- Edinburgh
- Florence
- Hong Kong
- Istanbul
- Las Vegas
- Lisbon
- London
- Madrid
- Milan
- Montréal
- Munich
- New York City
- Orlando
- Paris
- Rome
- San Francisco
- Seattle
- Shanghai
- Singapore
- Sydney
- Tokyo
- Toronto
- Venice
- Washington, D.C.